Office 2010
for the Over 50s

Prentice Hall
is an imprint of

Harlow, England • London • New York • Boston • San Francisco • Toronto • Sydney • Singapore • Hong Kong
Tokyo • Seoul • Taipei • New Delhi • Cape Town • Madrid • Mexico City • Amsterdam • Munich • Paris • Milan

Pearson Education Limited

Edinburgh Gate
Harlow CM20 2JE
Tel: +44 (0)1279 623623
Fax: +44 (0)1279 431059
Website: www.pearsoned.co.uk

First published in Great Britain in 2011

Pearson Education is not responsible for the content of third party internet sites.

ISBN: 978-0-273-74415-3

British Library Cataloguing-in-Publication Data
A catalogue record for this book is available from the British Library

Library of Congress Cataloging-in-Publication Data
Ballew, Joli.
   Office 2010 for the over 50s in simple steps / Joli Ballew. -- 1st ed.
       p. cm.
   ISBN 978-0-273-74415-3 (pbk.)
  1. Microsoft Office. 2. Business--Computer programs. I. Title.
   HF5548.4.M525B355 2010
   005.5--dc22
                                        2010040861

10 9 8 7 6 5 4 3 2 1
14 13 12 11 10

Designed by pentacorbig, High Wycombe
Typeset in 11/14 pt ITC Stone Sans by 3
Printed in Great Britain by Scotprint, Haddington.

Office 2010 for the Over 50s

in Simple steps

Joli Ballew

Use your computer with confidence

Get to grips with practical computing tasks with minimal time, fuss and bother.

In Simple Steps guides guarantee immediate results. They tell you everything you need to know on a specific application; from the most essential tasks to master, to every activity you'll want to accomplish, through to solving the most common problems you'll encounter.

Helpful features

To build your confidence and help you to get the most out of your computer, practical hints, tips and shortcuts feature on every page:

 ALERT: Explains and provides practical solutions to the most commonly encountered problems

 HOT TIP: Time and effort saving shortcuts

 SEE ALSO: Points you to other related tasks and information

 DID YOU KNOW? Additional features to explore

WHAT DOES THIS MEAN?

Jargon and technical terms explained in plain English

Practical. Simple. Fast.

Dedication:

For Jennifer, my favourite civil engineer; I love you!

Author's acknowledgements:

I am so thankful for the opportunities the folks at Pearson have given me; I've written over a dozen books in the *Brilliant* and *In Simple Steps* series, and they continue to come back to me for more. Steve Temblett, Katy Robinson, and the rest of the crew are fantastic to work with and they give me free rein over content and voice, and are encouraging at every turn.

I am particularly fond of the books in the *Over 50s* series. My readers are loyal, enthusiastic, and ready to learn, and as I always suggest, contact me when they're in trouble. Should you, dear reader, ever need a bit of encouragement or a solution to a simple computer problem, feel free to contact me at joli_ballew@hotmail.com. I answer all emails, and I'd love to hear from you.

I would like to acknowledge my family: Dad, Cosmo, Jennifer, and Andrew, and my extended family, Garth, Theresa, Doug, Laura, and Nathan. Hopefully, in a couple of years we'll have more names in this list by way of more grandchildren!

I also have a close relationship with my agent, Neil Salkind of the Salkind Literary Agency. I doubt an author in my field can often say that they have 'too much' work, but, on occasion, I have to say that to Neil. It's nice to continue to earn my income from writing, especially when I can do it at home and at my leisure. Thanks, Neil, I couldn't do it without you.

Finally, I have quite a few very dear friends who think I'm some sort of genius, even though I'm not. Just because I know a lot about computers doesn't mean I can spout off pi to 30 digits, tell you which way is north from where I'm standing, or what time it is in New York. I'm just plugging along like everyone else, working to make the world a better (and more knowledgeable) place.

in Simple
steps

Contents at a glance

Top 10 Office 2010 Tips for the Over 50s

1 Introduction to Microsoft Office 2010

- Create shortcuts to programs   20
- Open Office programs   21
- Explore the Ribbon   23
- Explore the File tab   25

2 Introduction to Microsoft Word

- Open a new, blank document   31
- Preview and apply a style   36
- Check spelling and grammar   43
- Save a document   47

3 Edit documents

- Open an existing document   51
- Select and replace text   52
- Add a comment   60
- Use Strikethrough   61

4 Share, print, and personalise

- Email a document   65
- Print a document   67
- Explore printer settings   68
- Change where files save by default   71

5 Introduction to Microsoft Outlook

- Start Outlook the first time and input email information   78
- Check for new emails   82
- Reply to or forward an email   88
- Compose a new email   89

6 Explore Calendar and contacts

- Add an appointment   110
- Set a reminder   112
- Add a contact   115
- Add a contact from an email   117

7 Print, personalise, back up, and explore

- Print an email   124
- Print a calendar   126
- Back up Outlook data   139
- Archive messages   143

8 Introduction to Microsoft Excel

- Open a new workbook from a template   147
- Input data into cells   149
- Edit the contents in a cell   153
- Save a workbook   155

9 Manage and edit workbooks

- Name or rename a worksheet 171
- Insert rows and columns 172
- Merge cells 174
- Write your own formula 180

10 Share, print, and personalise

- Save a workbook 185
- Protect a workbook 188
- Print a workbook 193
- Change where files save by default 194

11 Introduction to Microsoft PowerPoint

- Open a new presentation 203
- Add text to a slide 209
- Insert a picture 214
- Preview your slideshow 223

Top 10 Office 2010 Problems Solved

Contents

Top 10 Office 2010 Tips for the Over 50s

1	Create shortcuts to all Office programs	2
2	Use the Format Painter	3
3	Preview and apply a style in Word	4
4	Use Cut, Copy, and Paste	6
5	Browse available templates	7
6	Personalise the Quick Access Toolbar	8
7	Add a sender to Outlook's address book	10
8	Back up Outlook data	11
9	Insert a picture or clip art	13
10	Preview and apply a theme in PowerPoint	15

1 Introduction to Microsoft Office 2010

● Understand Office programs	19
● Create shortcuts to programs	20
● Open Office programs	21
● Explore the tabs	22
● Explore the Ribbon	23
● Explore the File tab	25
● Understand Office Options	27

2 Introduction to Microsoft Word

● Open a new, blank document	31
● Type a letter	32
● Apply font characteristics to text	34

● Preview and apply a style 36

● Create a bulleted or numbered list 38

● Insert a picture 39

● Insert clip art 40

● Edit a picture or clip art 41

● Use the Thesaurus 42

● Check spelling and grammar 43

● Choose a different view 45

● Use Zoom 46

● Save a document 47

● Get Help 48

3 Edit documents

● Open an existing document 51

● Select and replace text 52

● Use Cut, Copy, and Paste 53

● Use Undo Typing and Redo Typing 55

● Use Find and Replace 56

● Use the Format Painter 57

● Create a table 58

● Add a comment 60

● Use Strikethrough 61

4 Share, print, and personalise

● Email a document 65

● Save and send a document as a PDF 66

● Print a document 67

● Explore printer settings 68

● Print an envelope 69

● Print labels   70

● Change where files save by default   71

● Personalise the Quick Access Toolbar   72

● Learn more   74

5 Introduction to Microsoft Outlook

● Get a free email address   77

● Start Outlook the first time and input email information   78

● Input a secondary email account   80

● Set one account as the default account   81

● Check for new emails   82

● Stay in Mail view   83

● Read (and delete) an email   84

● Add a sender to the address book   85

● Change how often Outlook checks for emails   87

● Reply to or forward an email   88

● Compose a new email   89

● Explore advanced formatting options   91

● Attach a file   92

● Insert a picture   93

● Edit a picture   95

● Request receipts   97

● Preview an attachment   98

● Open and save attachments   99

● Use Zoom   100

● Keep your Inbox clean   101

● Empty Sent and Deleted Items folders   102

● Create folders   103

● Move mail into folders   105

6 Explore Calendar and contacts

- Explore Calendar view   109
- Add an appointment   110
- Set a reminder   112
- Explore Folder List view   113
- Browse contacts   114
- Add a contact   115
- Add a contact from an email   117
- Create a contact group   118

7 Print, personalise, back up, and explore

- Use Print Preview   123
- Print an email   124
- Print a calendar   126
- Search for an email   127
- Move the Quick Access Toolbar   129
- Add Print to the Quick Access Toolbar   130
- Add New E-mail to the Quick Access Toolbar   131
- Add a custom group   133
- Add your favourite commands to the custom group   135
- Remove an item from the Ribbon   137
- Understand the Outlook .pst file   138
- Back up Outlook data   139
- Export your address book   141
- Archive messages   143
- Learn more   144

8 Introduction to Microsoft Excel

- Open a new workbook from a template   147
- Input data into cells   149
- Use Zoom   150
- Make cell data easier to see   151
- Edit the contents in a cell   153
- View another worksheet   154
- Save a workbook   155
- Open a new, blank workbook   156
- Create headings for a monthly expenses budget   157
- Create budget categories   158
- Input budget approximations   159
- Get the sum of a column of numbers   160
- Get the average of a column of numbers   162
- Copy and paste a formula   164
- Get Help   165
- Opt for templates   167

9 Manage and edit workbooks

- Name or rename a worksheet   171
- Insert rows and columns   172
- Delete and hide rows and columns   173
- Merge cells   174
- Select a range of data   175
- Apply a conditional format to a range   176
- Convert a range to a bar chart   177
- Convert a range to a line chart   178

- Add titles and data labels to a chart 179
- Write your own formula 180
- Get help with formulas 181

10 Share, print, and personalise

- Save a workbook 185
- Change the file type 186
- Create a PDF document 187
- Protect a workbook 188
- Send a workbook in an email 189
- Use Print Preview 190
- Explore Page Setup 192
- Print a workbook 193
- Change where files save by default 194
- Personalise the Quick Access Toolbar 196
- Customise the Ribbon 197
- Learn more 199

11 Introduction to Microsoft PowerPoint

- Open a new presentation 203
- Explore templates 205
- Preview and apply a theme 207
- Add text to a slide 209
- Insert a text box 211
- Apply font characteristics to text 212
- Insert a picture 214
- Insert clip art 215
- Edit a picture or clip art 217

- Create a bulleted or numbered list   219
- Insert a hyperlink   220
- Create additional slides   221
- Apply a transition   222
- Preview your slideshow   223
- Get Help   224

Top 10 Office 2010 Problems Solved

1	Find a synonym for a word	226
2	Zoom in on anything	227
3	Create a greeting card, award certificate, budget sheet, or anything else, fast!	228
4	Configure Outlook to check for email more often	230
5	Insert and delete rows and columns in Excel	232
6	Change default settings in Office programs	234
7	Resolve printing issues	235
8	Resize, edit, or reposition pictures or clip art	236
9	Resolve a problem with an Excel formula	237
10	Resolve a problem that is not addressed here or in the book	239

Top 10 Office 2010 Tips for the Over 50s

1	Create shortcuts to all Office programs	2
2	Use the Format Painter	3
3	Preview and apply a style in Word	4
4	Use Cut, Copy, and Paste	6
5	Browse available templates	7
6	Personalise the Quick Access Toolbar	8
7	Add a sender to Outlook's address book	10
8	Back up Outlook data	11
9	Insert a picture or clip art	13
10	Preview and apply a theme in PowerPoint	15

Tip 1: Create shortcuts to all Office programs

To open a Microsoft Office program, you have to locate it on your computer. On a Windows 7 computer, this means you have to click Start, click All Programs, click Microsoft Office, and then click the program you want to use. Although you can go this way each time you want to open a program, it's easier to create shortcuts to these programs on your Taskbar, Start Menu, or the Desktop.

1 Locate the Microsoft Office Programs on your computer. On a Windows 7 PC:
   - Click Start and click All Programs.
   - Click Microsoft Office.

2 Right-click Microsoft Word 2010, point to Send to, and click Desktop (create shortcut).

3 Locate the new shortcut on your Desktop.

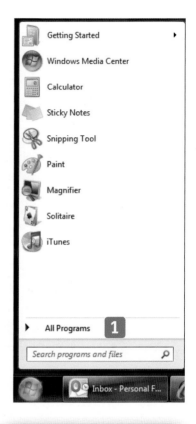

? DID YOU KNOW?
In Windows 7 you can also choose to pin the program to the Start menu or the Taskbar, if you'd rather create the shortcuts there instead of your Desktop.

🔥 HOT TIP: Create shortcuts for Word, Excel, Outlook, and PowerPoint so you can open them with a single or double-click.

Tip 2: Use the Format Painter

If you've applied formatting to a particular portion of a document, email, spreadsheet, or presentation and you want to copy that formatting and apply it to another part of the document, you use the Format Painter. It does just what you'd expect; it applies formatting you've copied.

1 In any file, apply various formatting to a particular part of the text. You may opt to underline, apply bold, and highlight, for instance.

2 Select the text.

3 From the Home screen, click Format Painter.

4 Drag the mouse, which now has a paintbrush beside the cursor, over the text to apply the formatting to it.

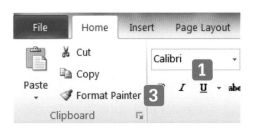

Use the Format Painter

If you've applied formatting to a particular portion of a docum
and apply it to another part of the text, you use the Format Pa
applies formatting you've copied.

1. In any Word document, apply various formatting to a p
underline, apply bold, and highlight, for instance.
2. Select the text.
3. From the Home screen, click **Format Painter**. ——**4**

? DID YOU KNOW?

If you decide not to apply formatting using Format Painter after clicking the Format Painter button, click with the mouse once to cancel.

🔥 HOT TIP: To apply the Format Painter again after applying it, start again at Step 2, or double-click the Format Painter button to apply the same formatting to multiple places in the document.

Tip 3: Preview and apply a style in Word

Styles, available from the Home tab in Word in the Styles *group*, offers preconfigured headings, titles, subtitles, and similar offerings. You can click to apply a style to quickly format text. For instance, you can apply the Title style to create a heading for a family reunion notice.

1 Type any text, in this case, a heading for a family reunion notice.

2 Select the text you want to apply the style to (by dragging your mouse over it while holding down the left mouse button).

3 Hover your mouse over any style to preview it.

4 To select and apply a style, click it.

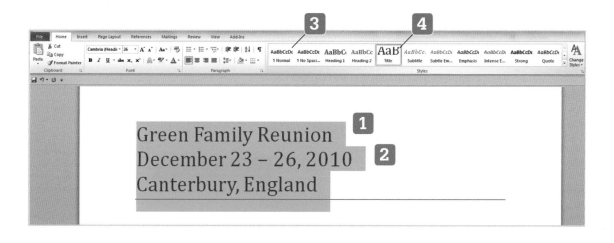

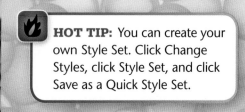

HOT TIP: You can create your own Style Set. Click Change Styles, click Style Set, and click Save as a Quick Style Set.

5 Continue adding text as desired. To apply a style to only one line of text, click to insert your cursor in that line if you'd rather not select the text.

Please RSVP by November 1st, 2010. **5**

? DID YOU KNOW?

There are lots of other Style "sets". To see them and switch to them, click the Change Styles button and then Style Set. You'll see the options here.

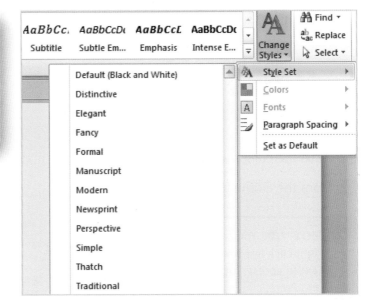

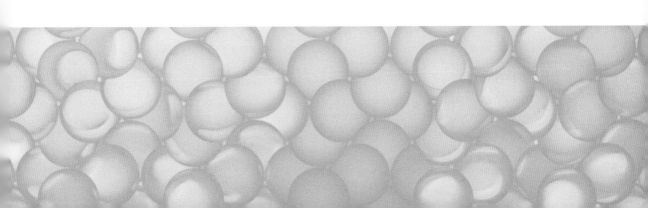

Tip 4: Use Cut, Copy, and Paste

You don't have time to take the long way around, you need to know shortcuts! Cut, Copy, and Paste are shortcuts you can use to remove, move, and/ or copy data.

1 Select any text in a document.

2 From the Home tab, click Cut or Copy. (Cut removes the text; Copy leaves it.)

3 Place the cursor where you'd like to paste the text.

4 From the Home tab, click Paste.

HOT TIP: You can also right-click any selected text to access Cut, Copy, and Paste.

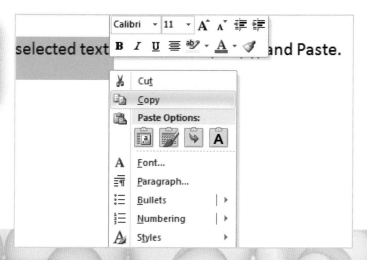

DID YOU KNOW?

You can copy data from any Office program and paste it just about anywhere, in an email, in Word, Excel, or PowerPoint, or even on the web.

DID YOU KNOW?

You can double-click to select a single word or triple-click to select an entire paragraph.

DID YOU KNOW?

Click the arrow next to Clipboard under the Home tab to see a list of items you've cut and copied. Click any item in the list to paste it.

Tip 5: Browse available templates

Templates are available from the File tab. Just click New. Some of the options under New are available from your computer, like Blank document and Blog post. All of the others are available from the internet, at Office.com.

1️⃣ In Word, Excel, or PowerPoint, click the File tab.

2️⃣ Click New.

3️⃣ Under the Office.com section, browse the available template categories.

4️⃣ Double-click any folder and note the subcategories. You can also preview any template in the right pane.

5️⃣ Click the Back button to return to the main categories.

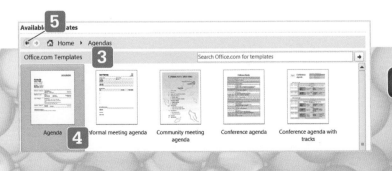

🔥 HOT TIP: If you're looking for something specific, type a keyword into the Search box and click the arrow to see what's available.

Tip 6: Personalise the Quick Access Toolbar

The Quick Access Toolbar is the small toolbar that appears above or below the Ribbon. It contains Save, Undo Typing, and Redo Typing. You can add commands there you use often. You may want to add Open recent file, E-mail, Print, or Cut, Copy, and Paste (which are dependent on the commands available in the program you're using).

1 Click the down arrow on the Quick Access Toolbar.

2 Click any command to add.

3 To add a command that isn't shown, click More Commands.

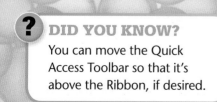

DID YOU KNOW?

You can move the Quick Access Toolbar so that it's above the Ribbon, if desired.

4 From the resulting dialog box, select any command in the left pane and click Add to add it to the Quick Access Toolbar. Here we're adding Format Painter.

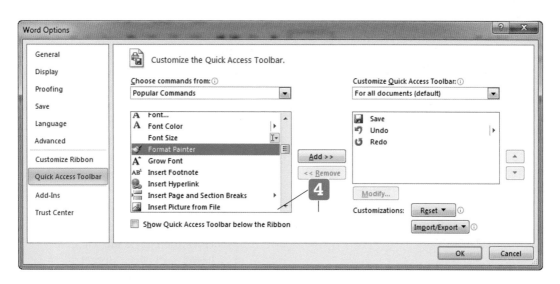

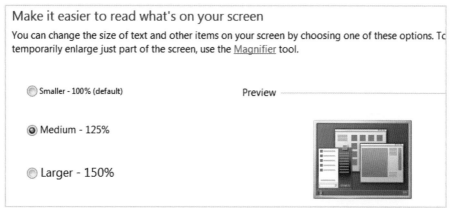

Make it easier to read what's on your screen

You can change the size of text and other items on your screen by choosing one of these options. To temporarily enlarge just part of the screen, use the Magnifier tool.

○ Smaller - 100% (default)

◉ Medium - 125%

Preview

○ Larger - 150%

🔥 **HOT TIP:** If the icons on the Quick Access Toolbar (or the Ribbon) are too small for you to see easily, change the display settings for your entire computer in Control Panel. Ours is set to 125%, which makes everything just a little bit larger.

🔥 **HOT TIP:** In the top figure above the most popular commands are listed for Word, however, you can click the down arrow to see more commands, organised by their respective tabs, and commands vary by program.

Tip 7: Add a sender to Outlook's address book

Your email addresses are stored in Outlook's Address Book. You can access your address book from the Home tab. Although there are several ways to get email addresses into the address book, adding them from an email you receive is the easiest.

1 After you receive an email, click it to select it.

2 In the Reading Pane, locate the sender's email address.

3 Right-click the address.

4 Click Add to Outlook Contacts.

5 Notice all of the available options for personalising the contacts, including the tabs. Type the desired information.

6 Click Save & Close.

HOT TIP: You can import email addresses you've acquired with other email programs from the File tab. Click Open and then Import. Choose Import Internet Mail and Addresses and follow the prompts.

DID YOU KNOW?
You can add a contact manually. From the Home tab, click New Items, and click Contact.

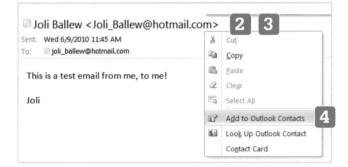

Tip 8: Back up Outlook data

Data you store in Outlook can be quite valuable. You have email messages and contacts of course, but you may also have pictures that came as attachments in emails, folders and subfolders you've created, receipts you're saving for tax time, lab results from doctors, and software codes for applications you've purchased online. If you lost it all, you'd have a time getting it all back; it's best to create a regular backup schedule.

1 Click the File tab, and click Open.

2 Click Import.

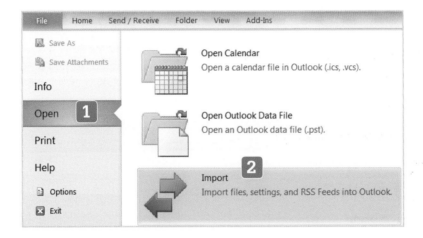

3 Click Export to a file; click Next.

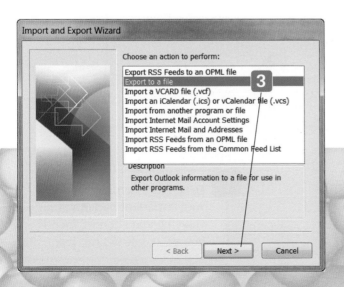

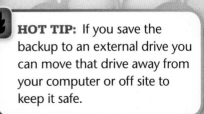

HOT TIP: If you save the backup to an external drive you can move that drive away from your computer or off site to keep it safe.

4 Click Outlook Data File (.pst) and click Next. (This is not shown.)

5 Click Personal Folders, verify Include subfolders is ticked, and click Next.

6 Click Browse.

7 Browse to the location to save the file, preferably an external drive or network drive.

8 Name the file and click OK.

9 Leave Replace duplicates with items imported selected and click Finish.

10 If desired, create a password when prompted and click OK.

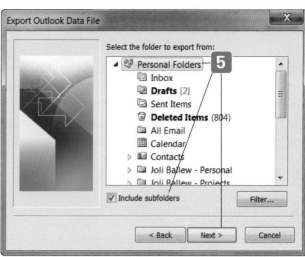

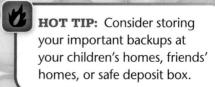
HOT TIP: If you don't have a backup drive available, save the file to your personal folder or the Desktop, and then drag it to a flash drive for safe keeping later.

HOT TIP: Consider storing your important backups at your children's homes, friends' homes, or safe deposit box.

Tip 9: Insert a picture or clip art

You can add pictures or clip art anywhere you like in any Word document, Excel worksheet, PowerPoint presentation, or new email.

1 Open any document or outgoing email you'd like to personalise with a picture or clip art.

2 Click inside the document, worksheet, slide, or email near where you'd like to add the image.

3 Click the Insert tab.

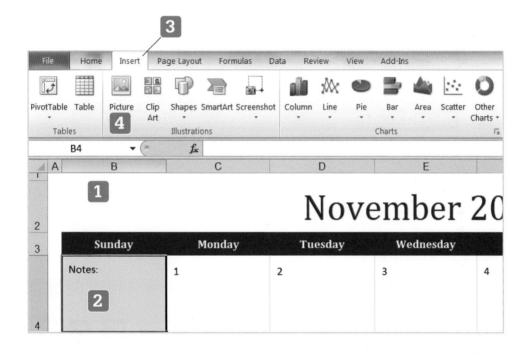

🔥 **HOT TIP:** Think about the documents, presentations, and worksheets you've already created and how you could enhance them with images. Invoices, home inventory lists, presentation slides, and outgoing email can all be personalised with pictures and clip art.

❓ **DID YOU KNOW?**
You move any image by clicking and dragging it, and you resize it by dragging from the corners. You can also edit images by clicking them once to select them, and then clicking the Picture Tools tab.

4 To add a picture:
- Click Picture.
- Browse to the location of the file, click it, and click Insert.
- Resize the image as needed.

5 To add clip art:
- Click Clip Art.
- Search for and locate the clip art to add.
- Double-click it.
- Resize as necessary.

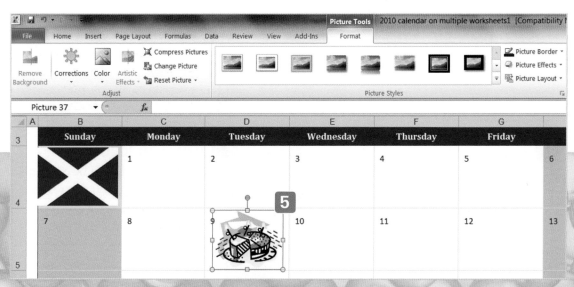

Tip 10: Preview and apply a theme in PowerPoint

You can apply a theme to an entire presentation in a couple of clicks of the mouse. Themes include background colours, graphics, and preconfigured fonts, font sizes, and matching font colours. You can create a presentation quickly and easily by selecting a theme right at the beginning.

1 Open a new, blank, PowerPoint presentation.

2 Click the Design tab.

3 Hover the mouse over the available themes to see their previews, and then click the arrow in the Themes group to see all of the options.

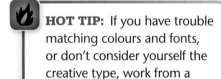

HOT TIP: If you have trouble matching colours and fonts, or don't consider yourself the creative type, work from a theme.

HOT TIP: PowerPoint comes with several themes, you can get more from Office.com, or you can browse for themes stored on your computer.

? DID YOU KNOW?
When you apply a theme, it will be applied to new slides you create for the current presentation.

HOT TIP: You can change the theme at any time, even after inputting text and images, and your data will remain intact (although its position, size, and features may change to incorporate the new theme's characteristics).

4 Drag from the bottom right corner to expand the window, if necessary.

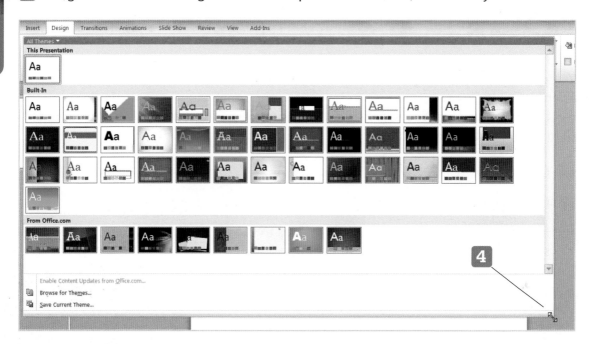

5 Click any theme to apply it.

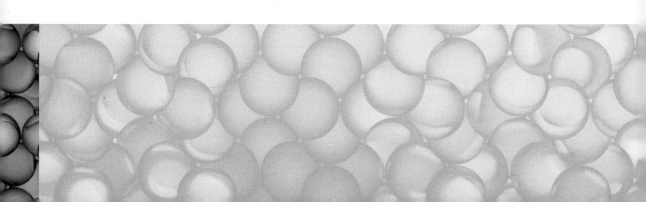

1 Introduction to Microsoft Office 2010

Understand Office programs   19

Create shortcuts to programs   20

Open Office programs   21

Explore the tabs   22

Explore the Ribbon   23

Explore the File tab   25

Understand Office Options   27

Introduction

Microsoft Office is a suite of productivity applications that enable you to create family newsletters, invitations, budget spreadsheets, and presentations, to maintain a calendar, and to send and receive email, among other things. The applications included in the suite vary depending on the edition you purchase, but all suites include Word, Excel, and PowerPoint. Most include Outlook as well. More expensive versions include applications such as Publisher, Access, Groove, and others. In this book, we'll cover Word, Excel, Outlook, and PowerPoint.

Once you learn to use these programs you can easily create flyers and brochures for public events, including those in your local community, signs for garage sales or lost pets, and invoices, time sheets, and schedules for a new venture. You can create household budget workbooks and spreadsheets, configure and maintain multiple calendars for multiple people in your home, and manage email, notes, and tasks with included organisational tools. You've made a good purchase and have taken a big step; let's get started!

Understand Office programs

The Microsoft Office Suite of applications in the Office Standard edition includes Word, Excel, Outlook, and PowerPoint. We'll cover these applications in this book. Each application is unique and can be used to perform tasks like creating leaflets, a financial plan, and a presentation for a retirement party, or to manage email.

- Microsoft Office Word – To create and edit documents including letters, flyers, brochures, and even novels. You can insert pictures and clip art to really add spice to the things you create too.

 HOT TIP: If you decide you want additional Microsoft Office applications, you can purchase them separately.

- Microsoft Office Excel – To enter, analyse, calculate, and manage data, including those related to budgets and loan payments, and you can even maintain simple databases.

- Microsoft Office Outlook – To manage all of your email and email accounts in one place, to maintain a calendar, to keep notes and create tasks and to-do lists.

- Microsoft Office PowerPoint – To create presentations with animations, transitions, pictures, music, and more for parties, community and civic events, and even friends or relatives.

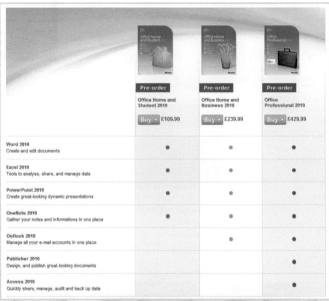

	Office Home and Student 2010	Office Home and Business 2010	Office Professional 2010
	Pre-order	Pre-order	Pre-order
	Buy ▾ £109.99	Buy ▾ £239.99	Buy ▾ £429.99
Word 2010 — Create and edit documents	●	●	●
Excel 2010 — Tools to analyse, share, and manage data	●	●	●
PowerPoint 2010 — Create great-looking dynamic presentations	●	●	●
OneNote 2010 — Gather your notes and informations in one place	●	●	●
Outlook 2010 — Manage all your e-mail accounts in one place		●	●
Publisher 2010 — Design, and publish great-looking documents			●
Access 2010 — Quickly share, manage, audit and back up data			●

 HOT TIP: You can compare editions of Microsoft Office online at the Microsoft Store.

 DID YOU KNOW?

Publisher is another application to consider. With it you can design and publish dynamic, professional-quality documents, including wedding invitations and professional announcements.

Create shortcuts to programs

To open a Microsoft Office program, you have to locate it on your computer. On a Windows 7 computer, this means you have to click Start, click All Programs, click Microsoft Office, and then click the program you want to use. Although you can do this each time you want to open a program, it's easier to create shortcuts to these programs on your Taskbar, Start Menu, or the Desktop, to save a little wear and tear on your mouse-clicking finger!

1 Locate the Microsoft Office Programs on your computer. On a Windows 7 PC:

- Click Start and click All Programs.
- Click Microsoft Office.

2 Right-click Microsoft Word 2010, point to Send to, and click Desktop (create shortcut).

3 Locate the new shortcut on your Desktop.

? **DID YOU KNOW?**

In Windows 7 you can also choose to pin the program to the Start menu or the Taskbar, if you'd rather create the shortcuts there instead of your Desktop.

🔥 **HOT TIP:** Create shortcuts for Word, Excel, Outlook, and PowerPoint so you can open them with a single or double-click.

Open Office programs

If you created shortcuts to your Office programs as outlined on the previous page, it'll be easy to open a program from the Desktop, Taskbar, or Start Menu, depending on the option you chose.

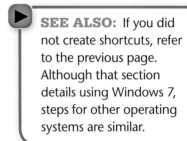 **SEE ALSO:** If you did not create shortcuts, refer to the previous page. Although that section details using Windows 7, steps for other operating systems are similar.

- If a shortcut exists on the Desktop, double-click it to open it.
- If you created a shortcut on the Start menu or Taskbar, click it once to open it.

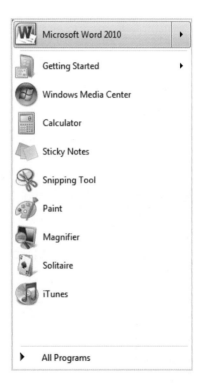

- If you did not create a shortcut, go into the Start and All Programs menu to find it. Click it once to open it.

 HOT TIP: If you pinned a program to the Start menu, hover your mouse over it to see the arrow and have access to recent documents.

 DID YOU KNOW?
The first time you open an Office program, you may be prompted to activate it online. If prompted, connect to the internet to complete this step.

Explore the tabs

Each Office program has tabs. You use these tabs to navigate in and around the program's window. You'll see a File tab, and, depending on the program, various other tabs, including perhaps Home, Insert, View, Page Layout, Review, and Design.

1 Open Microsoft Word.

2 Note the tabs at the top. Click each tab one at a time.

3 Review the items under each tab. Note that under Insert for instance, you can insert a picture.

4 Close Microsoft Word.

5 Open Microsoft PowerPoint.

6 Repeat the steps above. Note again the Insert tab and that programs in the suite have commonalities.

7 Repeat with Microsoft Excel (but not Microsoft Outlook).

? DID YOU KNOW?
If you insert a picture into a document and select it, a new tab will appear with picture tools. If you insert a table and select it, a new tab will appear with table tools.

! ALERT: Microsoft Outlook stands out from the other three programs we'll discuss in this book, and does not have most of the tabs you'll see in other applications.

Explore the Ribbon

The Ribbon is the part of the interface that appears underneath a selected tab. The tools on the Ribbon change each time you select a new tab. For instance, when you click the Home tab, in Word, Excel, and PowerPoint, you'll have options to format text, among other things. Under Insert, you'll see options to insert pictures and clip art, charts, tables, and similar items.

1 Open Microsoft Word and click the Home tab. Note the options to format text and change styles.

2 On the Home tab, notice the down-facing arrow in each of the tab sections. Click the one in the Font group to see additional font options. (Click Cancel to close this window.)

HOT TIP: The best way to familiarise yourself with the Ribbon and its components is to open the four programs and click each tab one at a time and note the tools available when you do.

3 In Microsoft Word, click the Insert tab. Note the options to insert elements including page numbers and tables.

4 Continue working through the tabs, noting what's available in each and how the Ribbon changes. Word's View menu is shown here.

5 Repeat with Excel, Outlook (see Alert), and PowerPoint, if desired.

Explore the File tab

Every program we'll discuss in the book has a File tab, just as each has a Home tab. The File tab is quite different from the rest of the tabs, though, and does not open a new selection on the Ribbon, but instead opens a new view with options for saving, opening, printing, sending, and configuring options for the program.

1 Open PowerPoint and click the File tab.

2 Click New, and take a look at all of the templates you can choose from when creating a presentation.

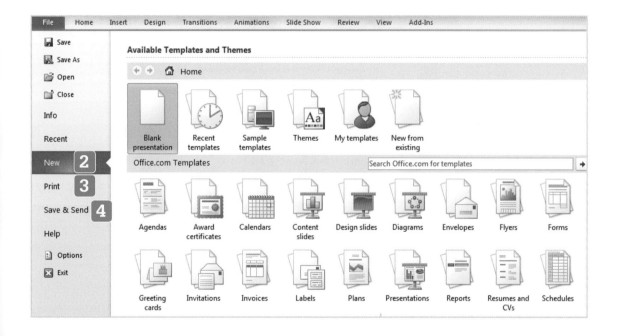

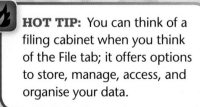

HOT TIP: You can think of a filing cabinet when you think of the File tab; it offers options to store, manage, access, and organise your data.

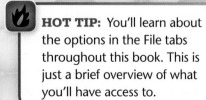

HOT TIP: You'll learn about the options in the File tabs throughout this book. This is just a brief overview of what you'll have access to.

3 Click Print. Note all the print options.

4 Click Save & Send. Note the various save and send options.

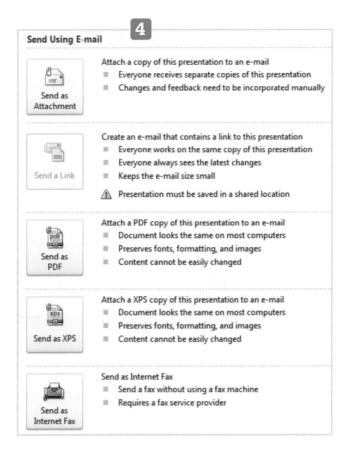

Understand Office Options

When you click the File tab in any Office application and then click Options, a dialog box will appear with options you can configure for that specific program. For instance in Outlook, you can configure how often Outlook should check for new email, or how the Calendar should display your week. (Not all people work Monday to Friday, from 8 a.m. to 5 p.m.)

1 Open Microsoft Word, and click the File tab.

2 Click Options.

3 Click Advanced.

4 Read through the Advanced options.

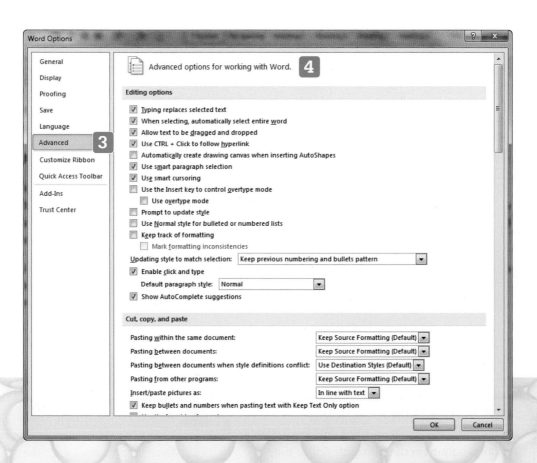

5 Explore Advanced options in Excel and PowerPoint.

6 If desired, in the Options window of any program, explore General, Proofing, Save, and other available tabs. Under General, choose a new Color Scheme if you find the current colour of Office distracting.

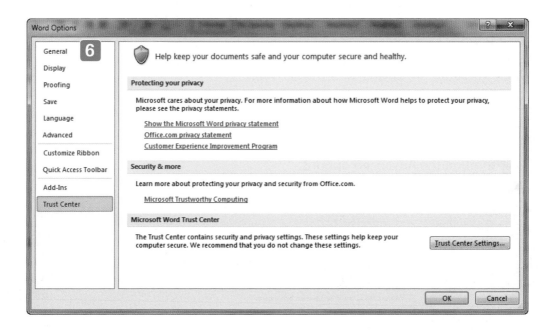

 **DID YOU KNOW?**

There are commonalities in the options available for all programs in the Microsoft Office suite including the ability to customise the Ribbon, change where files are saved by default, and configure the Quick Access Toolbar.

ALERT: The goal in this section is only to view and familiarise yourself with the Options dialog box. The goal is not to fully understand these options.

2 Introduction to Microsoft Word

Open a new, blank document	31
Type a letter	32
Apply font characteristics to text	34
Preview and apply a style	36
Create a bulleted or numbered list	38
Insert a picture	39
Insert clip art	40
Edit a picture or clip art	41
Use the Thesaurus	42
Check spelling and grammar	43
Choose a different view	45
Use Zoom	46
Save a document	47
Get Help	48

Introduction

Microsoft Word is a program you use to create Word documents. Documents can be created for just about anything, including simple letters or faxes, signs for lost pets or items for sale, family newsletters (complete with pictures), multipage brochures for a new product or business, or a playbill for a production at the local community centre. Because you can easily copy and paste, you can also create your own itineraries for travel, complete with pictures you copy from web sites. There's no end to what you can produce.

Microsoft Word, like the other applications in the Microsoft Office suite, has tabs across the top of the page and a Ribbon that changes each time you select one. There are tabs that enable you to save, open, and print documents (File), format text and align paragraphs (Home), insert pictures, clip art, shapes, and the like (Insert), and more.

Open a new, blank document

The first step in creating anything is to open Microsoft Word. When you do, a new, blank document will automatically appear. However, you can also open a new document from the File tab, something you'll explore here.

1 Open Microsoft Word. If you created a shortcut as detailed in Chapter 1, it should be on the Desktop, Taskbar, or Start menu.

2 Notice the new, blank document that appears, and notice the tabs across the top of the page.

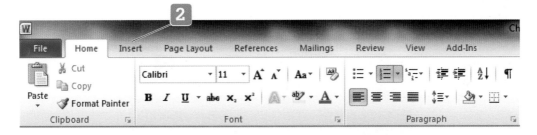

3 Click the File tab.

4 Click New.

5 Double-click Blank document, after scanning the other document options (Blog post, Agendas, Award certificates, etc.)

> **SEE ALSO:** If you do not have a shortcut for Microsoft Word on your Desktop, refer to Chapter 1 to learn how to create one.

> **? DID YOU KNOW?**
> You must be connected to the internet to access the Office.com templates, and after locating one you like, you must download it to your computer before you can use it. (Don't worry, downloading templates is safe!)

Type a letter

Many organisations and companies don't offer or accept email as a communication option and require you type a letter if you have a request or grievance. You may be required to type a letter to communicate with a doctor or insurance company, to send information to a bank, or to file a complaint with a restaurant, company, or public official.

1 Open Microsoft Word and start with a new, blank document.

2 Use the slider at the bottom of the interface to change how large the document appears on your screen. Try 100%, 150%, and 200%.

? DID YOU KNOW?

When writing a letter you should type your name and address at the top of the page, and the recipient's name and address below it. You can also add additional contact information if desired, and you should include the date. It's still the same technique you learned at school.

🔥 HOT TIP: Leave blank lines in between the paragraphs to make the letter easier to read. To add space, tap the Return or Enter key twice at the end of a paragraph.

? DID YOU KNOW?

If you make a typing mistake, look for the Undo button on the Quick Access Toolbar.

3 Click inside the document and begin typing.

4 Input a greeting, such as To Whom it May Concern:, and then type the body of the letter.

5 End the letter with a closing, such as Thank you or Yours sincerely, followed by your typed name. Sign the letter after printing it.

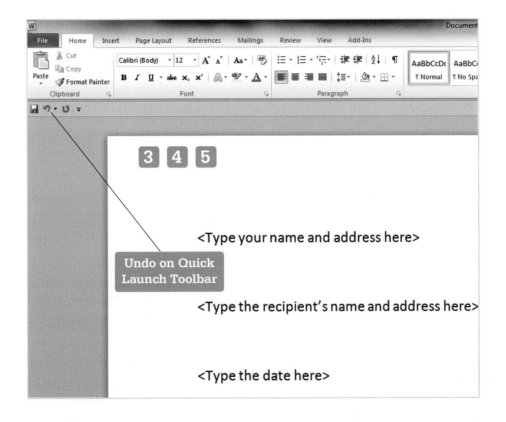

Apply font characteristics to text

You can apply font characteristics to text to draw attention to a specific part of the text or enlarge the font to make it easier for the recipient (or for you) to read. You can also highlight, underline, and even centre text (perhaps to create a professional-looking letterhead). You'll find all of these things from the Home tab.

1 Select the text to apply font characteristics to.

2 If the Home tab is not selected, click it.

3 Click the following to see the changes, and select the characteristics you'd like to apply:

- Click Bold.
- Click Italic.
- Click Underline.

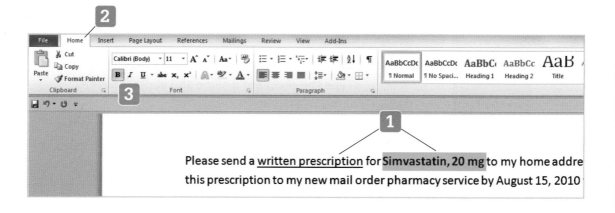

4 Click the arrow next to the font type to choose another font; click the arrow next to the font size to increase or decrease the font.

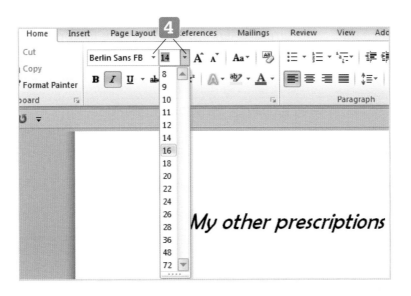

Preview and apply a style

Styles, available from the Home tab in Word in the Styles *group*, offers preconfigured headings, titles, subtitles, and similar offerings. You can click to apply a style to quickly format text. For instance, you can apply the Title style to create a heading for a family reunion notice.

1 Type any text, in this case, a heading for a family reunion notice.

2 Select the text you want to apply the style to (by dragging your mouse over it while holding down the left mouse button).

3 Hover your mouse over any style to preview it.

4 To select and apply a style, click it.

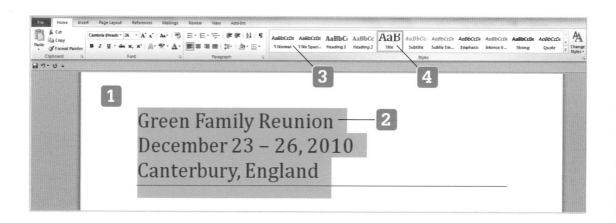

WHAT DOES THIS MEAN?

Group: A section of a tab that contains commands that are related to each other.

5 Continue adding text as desired. To apply a style to only one line of text, click to insert your cursor in that line if you'd rather not select the text.

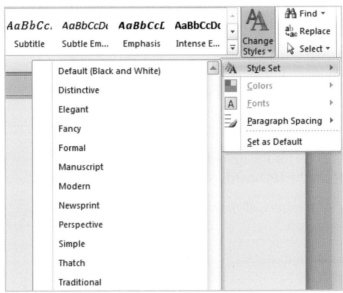

Create a bulleted or numbered list

Bulleted and numbered lists can help you organise data in a document. Generally, numbered lists are used to denote the order in which something must be done, while bulleted lists are reserved for features, options, or lists of things that can be done or viewed in any order.

1 In any document, from the Home tab, in the Paragraph group, click the Numbering icon.

2 A number will appear and an arrow beside it. You can click the arrow to see any available options, such as to continue numbering if a previous list exists in the document.

3 Type the information for the item and click Return or Enter on the keyboard.

4 To stop applying numbers, click the Numbering icon again.

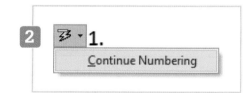

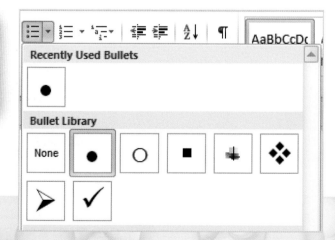

HOT TIP: To create a bulleted list instead, click the Bullets icon to the left of the Numbering icon.

Insert a picture

There will be times you'll want to insert a picture into your document. You may want to insert a picture of a lost dog, a caravan you want to sell, the cast of a play you're directing, or the damage done to your boat during a hail storm.

? DID YOU KNOW?

You can get pictures on to your computer by inserting a memory card into an available card slot, connecting a digital camera, or saving a picture from an email attachment.

1 Place the cursor in your document near where you'd like to insert the picture.

2 Click the Insert tab.

3 Click Picture.

4 Locate the picture on your computer and click Insert.

🔥 HOT TIP: To preview pictures as shown here, change the View in the window to Extra Large Icons.

? DID YOU KNOW?

Windows 7 prompts you to save pictures you upload from a digital camera to the Pictures folder. If you aren't sure where a picture is, look there.

Insert clip art

A piece of clip art is a digital, premade image. Clip art can be used in documents, spreadsheets, presentations, and the like, to add pizzazz. Microsoft Word comes with some clip art, but most of the clip art you'll have access to is on Office.com. So, when browsing for clip art, make sure you're connected to the internet.

1 Place the cursor in your document near where you'd like to insert the graphic.

2 Click the Insert tab.

3 Click Clip Art.

4 If prompted to include data from Office.com, do so.

5 Type a related term in the Search for: window and click Go.

6 Double-click any clip art to insert it into your document.

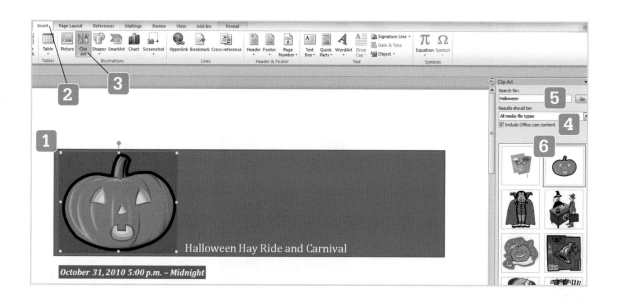

WHAT DOES THIS MEAN?

Office.com: An online repository of clip art, Help files, and more, managed by Microsoft to enhance productivity with Microsoft Office products.

? DID YOU KNOW?

You can also drag any clip art from the sidebar to the document.

Edit a picture or clip art

After you've inserted a picture or clip art, you will probably find some reason to edit it. It may be too large or too small, you may want to align it with existing text, add a border, or change the brightness or contrast. You access editing options from the Picture Tools tab, which appears when you click the clip art or image.

1 Click the picture or clip art you inserted in the previous section.

2 Click the Picture Tools tab.

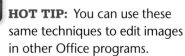

HOT TIP: You can use these same techniques to edit images in other Office programs.

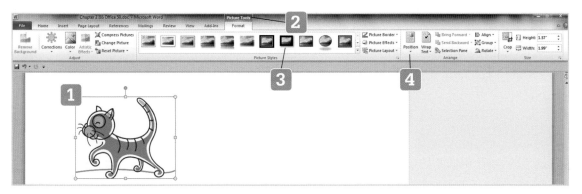

3 From the Picture Styles group, click any border.

4 To change how the picture aligns with the text, click Position and select any option.

5 To apply an effect, click Picture Effects and explore the options.

6 Continue editing as desired.

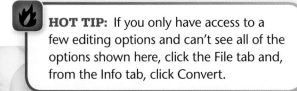

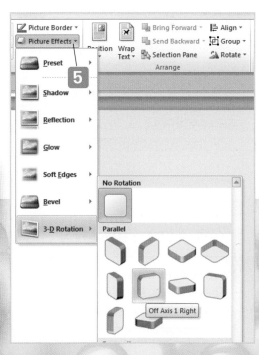

HOT TIP: If you only have access to a few editing options and can't see all of the options shown here, click the File tab and, from the Info tab, click Convert.

ALERT: If you can't see all of the features on any Ribbon, maximise the Word window so it takes up the entire screen.

Use the Thesaurus

OK, our minds aren't what they used to be. We're sure you've had a word on the tip of your tongue but been unable to come up with it. This is when the Thesaurus comes in handy. Of course, you can use it when you don't know the definition of a word too, or when you've used a word too many times in a paragraph and need an alternative.

1 Place your cursor inside a word you'd like to find an alternative for, learn the definition of, or replace.

2 Right-click with the mouse.

3 Click Synonyms.

4 Click the word you want to use to replace the selected word or click outside the menu to cancel.

? DID YOU KNOW?
Not all words will have available synonyms.

🔥 HOT TIP: If a word has a hyphen in it, select the entire word before right-clicking.

? DID YOU KNOW?
You can also access the Thesaurus from the Review tab. From here you can type a word to search for options.

Check spelling and grammar

When you type, Word will draw a line under any word you misspell. You can right-click the word to see the suggestions for correcting it. If you like the word the way it is spelled, right-click and choose Ignore or Add to Dictionary.

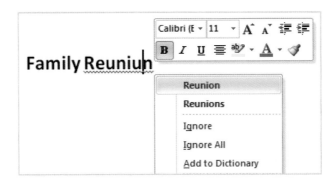

1   Click the Review tab.

2   Click Spelling and Grammar.

 **DID YOU KNOW?**
The Dictionary even includes newfangled tech words like *blog* and *Bluetooth*.

 HOT TIP: You can also check the spelling and grammar in an entire letter or document.

3 Work through the mistakes, accepting, changing, or ignoring what Word finds.

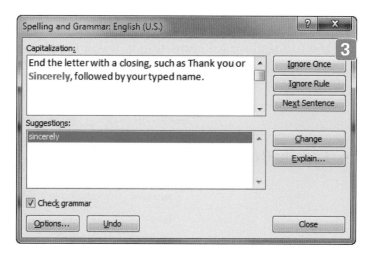

Spelling and Grammar: English (U.S.)

3

Capitalization:

End the letter with a closing, such as Thank you or
Sincerely, followed by your typed name.

Ignore Once

Ignore Rule

Next Sentence

Suggestions:

sincerely

Change

Explain...

☑ Check grammar

Options...   Undo

Close

4 Click Close when finished.

? **DID YOU KNOW?**

The Spelling and Grammar tool can also offer 'readability statistics' with information about the number of passive sentences, number of words, and even what level you're writing on. You have to enable this feature from the File tab, under Options, and in Proofing.

? **DID YOU KNOW?**

To set the Proofing language, click the Review tab and click Language. Here the language chosen was U.S.

Choose a different view

Word offers several ways to view documents on your computer screen. There's Print Layout, Full Screen Reading, Web Layout, Outline, and Draft, and you can opt to show or hide the Ruler, gridlines, or the Navigation Pane. You may find you prefer one view over another for specific tasks.

1 In any document, click the View tab.

2 Click Print Layout. This is how the page will look when printed.

HOT TIP: Print Layout seems to be the best view for composing a document, flyer, or brochure.

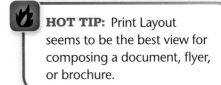

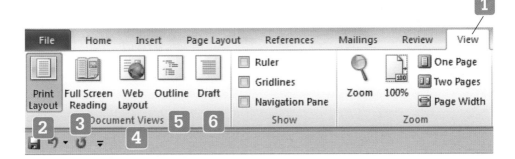

3 Click Full Screen Reading. This is just for reading, not editing or writing. Click the Esc key to return to the previous view.

4 Click Web Layout. This is how the page will look as a web page.

5 Click Outline. Click Close Outline view to close it.

6 Click Draft. Click Print Layout to return to the previous view.

7 Click Ruler, Gridlines, and Navigation Pane, then deselect these options.

HOT TIP: Try Outline view if your document has headings and subheadings and you want to review the hierarchy of heads.

HOT TIP: Show the Ruler when you need to align pictures or clip art.

45

Use Zoom

If you're having trouble seeing what's on the screen you can use the slider across the bottom to increase the page width. You can also use Zoom. Zoom lets you increase the size by a specific percentage.

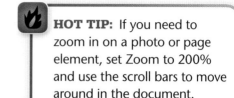

HOT TIP: If you need to zoom in on a photo or page element, set Zoom to 200% and use the scroll bars to move around in the document.

1 From the View tab, click Zoom.

2 Experiment with different Zoom views, clicking OK to apply.

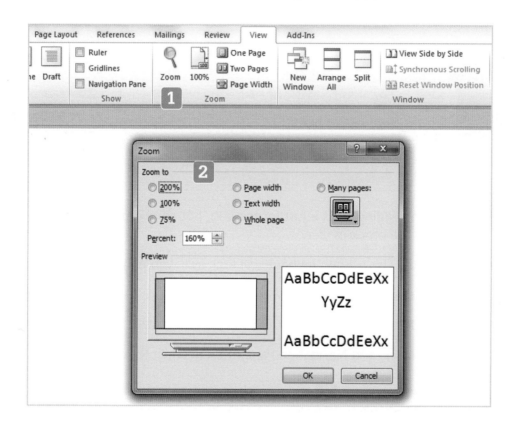

HOT TIP: If you click 75% you can often view the document two pages at a time; at 200% the text will take up more than the entire page.

DID YOU KNOW?
If you have two documents open at the same time, you can view them side by side. Side by Side is an option from the View tab.

Save a document

If you want to access your document later you'll need to save it. When you save a file it remains on your computer's hard drive until you delete it. Documents should be saved in your Documents folder or subfolders you've created within it.

1 Click the File tab.

2 Click Save As.

3 Browse to the location on your computer where you'd like to save the file.

4 Type a name for the file.

5 Click Save.

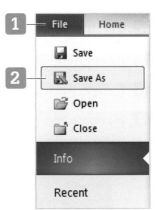

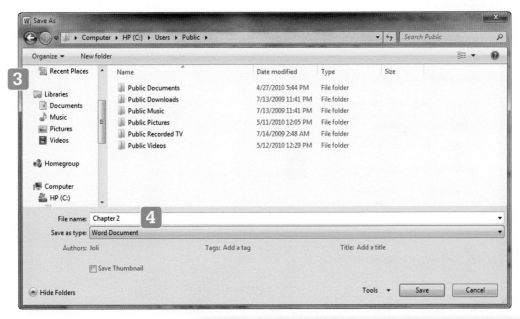

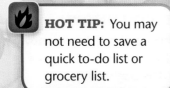

HOT TIP: You may not need to save a quick to-do list or grocery list.

? DID YOU KNOW?

There are lots of file formats available for saving Word documents. The default format is the Word Document format, but this format is not compatible with versions of Word before Word 2007 unless the user downloads the 'Word Viewer', a free add-on. If you want to save in another format, click the arrow next to Word Document to select a different option.

Get Help

There's an icon on the the far right side of the Ribbon that is a blue question mark. That's the Help icon. Click it to access the Microsoft Office Help files. If you're ever stuck and want a quick answer, this is the place to find it.

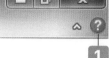

1 Click the blue icon on the Ribbon or press F1 on your keyboard.

2 If necessary, drag from the corner of the Help window to resize it.

3 Browse the available Help files or type a search word into the Search window.

4 Navigate the Help files as you would navigate a web page, by clicking links and using the Back and Forward buttons.

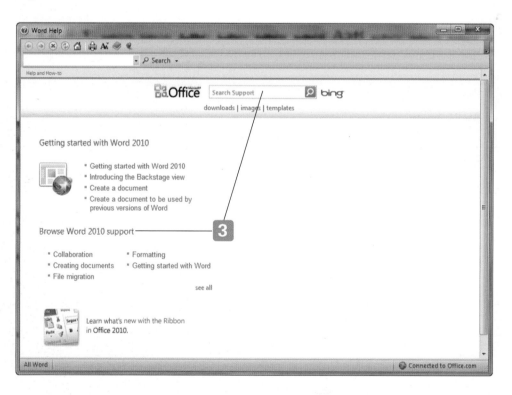

HOT TIP: To access all of the available Help files, connect to the internet. Most of the Help files are at Office.com.

DID YOU KNOW?
At the top of the Help window is a Print icon. Click it to print any Help page or topic.

3 Edit documents

Open an existing document   51

Select and replace text   52

Use Cut, Copy, and Paste   53

Use Undo Typing and Redo Typing   55

Use Find and Replace   56

Use the Format Painter   57

Create a table   58

Add a comment   60

Use Strikethrough   61

Introduction

Microsoft Word offers easy tools for editing documents. You can select and replace text or use Cut, Copy, and Paste to move data. There are options for Undo Typing and Redo Typing on the Quick Access Toolbar. You can use Find and Replace to locate and replace all instances of one word with another too. The latter is nice when you decide to change a character's name in a book you're writing, or when someone else decides to change the name of a golf tournament you're in charge of promoting.

You also have access to various tools for making your documents stand out. Word offers easy options for creating tables, and it's not at all complicated (as you might expect). Tables make it easy to organise and align data. You can edit others' work by adding comments, crossing out or deleting text and replacing it with something else, or even applying formatting to spice it up. There are lots of ways to edit documents, and here we'll touch on the basics.

Open an existing document

There are hundreds of reasons to open a document you've worked on previously: you forgot to add something important, you need to make a change to an event's date or time, you want to cross off or add things to a to-do or shopping list, you've found a new relative to add to a family tree, or you're ready to start a new chapter in a book or add another page to a newsletter.

1 Open Microsoft Word and click the File tab.

2 Click Open.

3 Locate the file to open. You may have to browse to it, but if you've saved it in the Documents folder, it may be available without browsing.

4 Click Open.

? **DID YOU KNOW?**

Your documents are probably saved in the Documents, My Documents, or Public Documents folders on your computer. If you're using Windows 7, check the Documents Library.

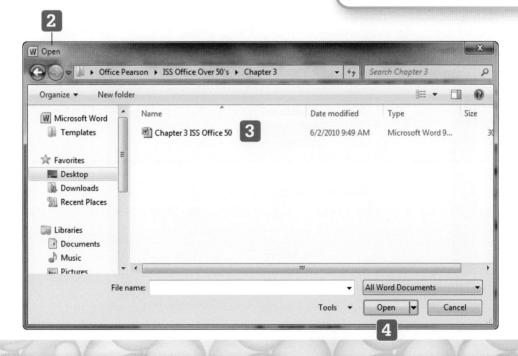

? **DID YOU KNOW?**

You can create folders inside folders to organise your documents. As you can see in the figure, the option New Folder is available. Click it to add a new organisational folder inside any folder.

HOT TIP: In Step 2, instead of clicking Open, click Recent. You'll see a list of all your recent documents there. Click to open any document in the list.

Select and replace text

In days past, if you typed a flyer or brochure with a typewriter and then found out a few days later you needed to change some of the wording in it, you had to retype the entire letter. You couldn't put the page back in the typewriter and remove and retype the text successfully (although we've all tried). Now, you simply open the file on your computer, select the text, and replace it. Simple!

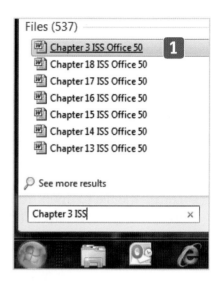

1 Open any file that needs editing.

2 Select the text to replace.

3 Type the replacement words.

HOT TIP: If you use Windows 7 or Vista, you can type the name of the file you want to open in the Start Search window, and from the results, click it to open.

Use Cut, Copy, and Paste

You don't have time to take the long way around, you need to know shortcuts! Cut, Copy, and Paste are shortcuts you can use to remove, move, and/or copy data.

1 Select any text in a document.

2 From the Home tab, click Cut or Copy. (Cut removes the text; Copy leaves it.)

3 Place the cursor where you'd like to paste the text.

4 From the Home tab, click Paste or right-click to paste, as shown below.

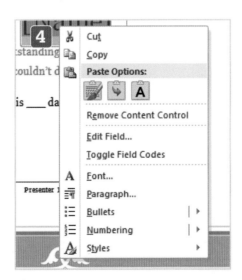

? **DID YOU KNOW?**

You can double-click to select a single word or triple-click to select an entire paragraph.

? **DID YOU KNOW?**

You can copy data from Microsoft Word and paste it just about anywhere, in an email, in Excel, in PowerPoint, or even on the web.

WHAT DOES THIS MEAN?

Cut: To remove text so that you can place it (paste it) somewhere else. (To delete text without the option of pasting later, select it and then click Delete on the keyboard.)

Copy: To copy text so that you can place it (paste it) somewhere else. The original text remains in place.

Paste: To insert text somewhere else that you've previously cut or copied (the same document, a new document, an email, a presentation, or just about anywhere).

 DID YOU KNOW?

Click the arrow next to Clipboard under the Home tab to see a list of items you've cut and copied. Click any item in the list to paste it.

 HOT TIP: You can right-click any selected text to access Cut, Copy, and Paste.

Use Undo Typing and Redo Typing

The Quick Access Toolbar is the toolbar that contains the icons for Save, Undo Typing, and Repeat Typing. The Undo Typing command lets you, well, undo the latest words you've typed. You can click Undo repeatedly, because Word keeps track of a long list of past edits. You can use Repeat Typing to undo an 'Undo Typing' command or to retype something you've previously typed.

1 In any Word document, type some text.

2 Click the Undo Typing button.

3 Click the Undo Typing button again.

4 Click Redo Typing.

5 Click the arrow next to Undo Typing.

6 Use your mouse to select multiple Undo points.

7 Click the last one selected to undo all previous typing to that point. (Click Redo Typing continuously to put it back.)

? DID YOU KNOW?

Undo Typing is not available when you first open a document, even if there's text in it and you've obviously typed something on a previous occasion. Undo Typing is only available on your latest edits to the document during a single writing session.

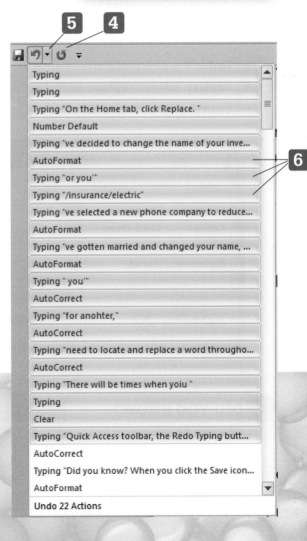

Typing
Typing
Typing "On the Home tab, click Replace. "
Number Default
Typing "ve decided to change the name of your inve...
AutoFormat
Typing "or you'"
Typing "/insurance/electric"
Typing "ve selected a new phone company to reduce...
AutoFormat
Typing "ve gotten married and changed your name, ...
AutoFormat
Typing " you'"
AutoCorrect
Typing "for anohter,"
AutoCorrect
Typing "need to locate and replace a word througho...
AutoCorrect
Typing "There will be times when yoiu "
Typing
Clear
Typing "Quick Access toolbar, the Redo Typing butt...
AutoCorrect
Typing "Did you know? When you click the Save icon...
AutoFormat
Undo 22 Actions

? DID YOU KNOW?

When you click the Save icon on the Quick Access Toolbar, the Redo Typing button becomes greyed out until you type something again.

Use Find and Replace

There will be times when you need to locate and replace a word throughout an entire document. Perhaps one cast member has been substituted for another, you've married and changed your name, you've selected a new phone/insurance/electricity company to reduce budget costs, or you've decided to change the name of your invention or business.

1 On the Home tab, click Replace.

2 Type what you'd like to find in Find what:, and type what you'd like to replace it with in Replace with:.

3 Click More to access more options.

4 Click any of the following:

- Find Next – to find the next instance of the word(s) and then choose to replace it or not.
- Replace – to replace an instance of a word(s) you've found using Find Next.
- Replace All – to replace all instances of the word(s) in the document.
- Cancel – to close the window and not make any changes.

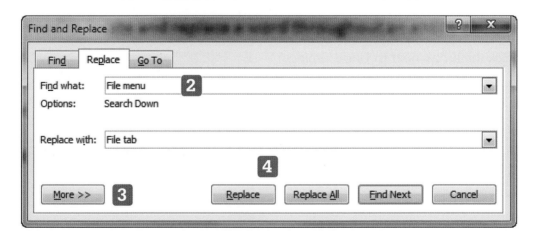

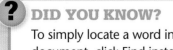

? DID YOU KNOW?

To simply locate a word in a document, click Find instead of Replace in Step 1.

🔥 HOT TIP: You can use the Undo Typing button to undo changes using Find and Replace.

Use the Format Painter

If you've applied formatting to a particular portion of a document and you want to copy that formatting and apply it to another part of the document, you use the Format Painter. It does just what you'd expect; it applies formatting you've copied.

1 In any Word document, apply various formatting to a particular part of the text. You may opt to underline, apply bold, and highlight, for instance.

2 Select the text.

3 From the Home screen, click Format Painter.

4 Drag the mouse, which now has a paintbrush beside the cursor, over the text to apply the formatting to it.

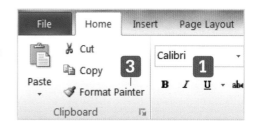

2 <u>**Use the Format Painter**</u>

If you've applied formatting to a particular portion of a docum
and apply it to another part of the text, you use the Format Pa
applies formatting you've copied.

1. In any Word document, apply various formatting to a p
   underline, apply bold, and highlight, for instance.
2. Select the text.
3. From the Home screen, click <u>**Format Painter**</u>. ⎯ **4**

 DID YOU KNOW?
If you decide not to apply formatting using Format Painter after clicking the Format Painter button, click with the mouse once to cancel.

HOT TIP: You can use the Format Painter to copy the formatting applied to numbered and bulleted lists.

Create a table

Word enables you to create tables easily. You can create tables for names, addresses, and birthdays; projects and supplies; problems and solutions. Tables allow you to easily organise data of all types.

1 In Word, click the Insert tab.

2 Click Table and use the mouse to create the table size.

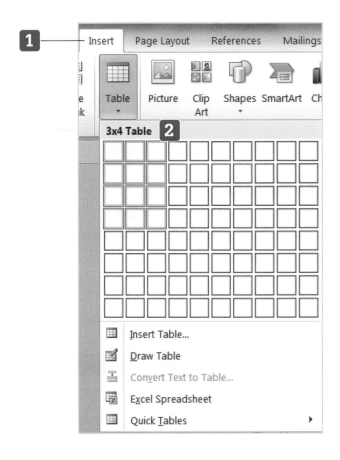

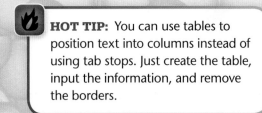

HOT TIP: You can use tables to position text into columns instead of using tab stops. Just create the table, input the information, and remove the borders.

3 Type data into the table as desired, using the Tab key to move between cells.

4 To insert additional rows or columns, place your cursor where you'd like to add this in the table, right-click, and select the desired option. In this case, we're using Insert, Rows below.

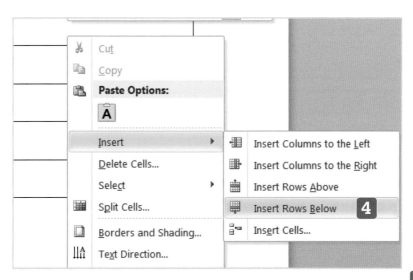

5 To remove borders (or to change them), place your cursor inside the table, and from the Table Tools, Design tab, select the desired border.

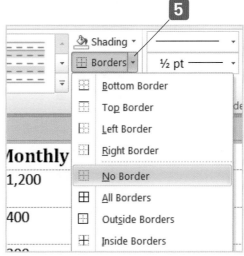

Add a comment

If you are ever asked to edit another person's work, perhaps for the purpose of proofreading it for publication or to offer suggestions, you'll want to insert comments. A comment appears on the document but not in it, as shown here.

1 Click the Review tab.

2 Highlight any text.

3 Click New Comment.

4 Type the comment.

5 Click outside the comment to continue working.

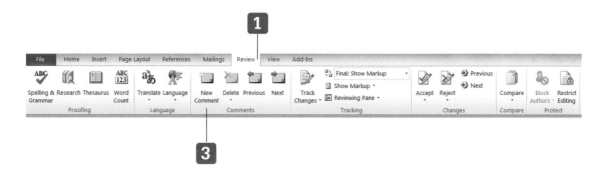

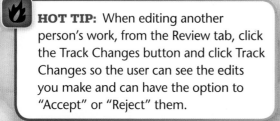

HOT TIP: When editing another person's work, from the Review tab, click the Track Changes button and click Track Changes so the user can see the edits you make and can have the option to "Accept" or "Reject" them.

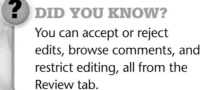

? DID YOU KNOW?

You can accept or reject edits, browse comments, and restrict editing, all from the Review tab.

Use Strikethrough

Strikethrough is a simple work formatting option from the Home tab. You can use the strikethrough feature to make sure your readers know that the text has been changed and is no longer applicable.

1 Highlight text you'd like to strike through.

2 Click the Strikethrough option on the Home tab in the Font group.

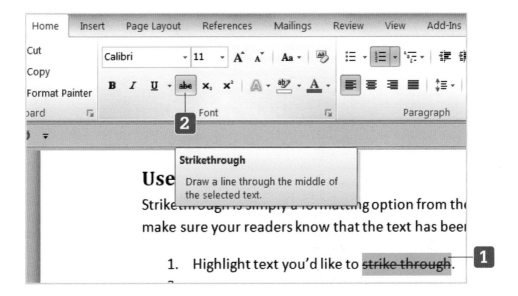

3 Highlight additional text.

? **DID YOU KNOW?**

You can apply almost all of the techniques you learned in this chapter to other Microsoft programs.

4 Click the arrow in the bottom right corner of the Font group on the Home tab.

5 Notice the additional options, including Double strikethrough.

6 Select any option to apply it, then click OK.

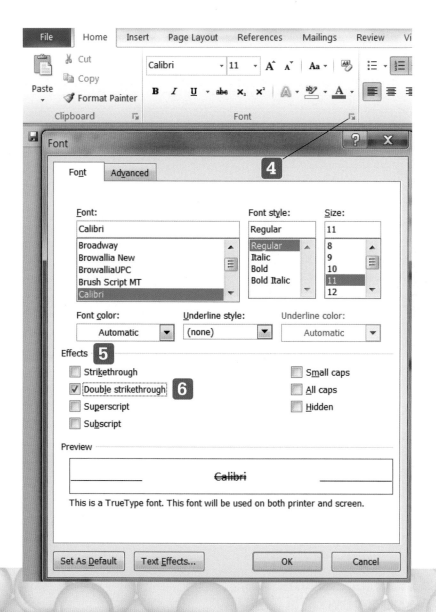

HOT TIP: Explore the other formatting options in the dialog box including Double Strikethrough and Hidden.

4 Share, print, and Personalise

Email a document	65
Save and send a document as a PDF	66
Print a document	67
Explore printer settings	68
Print an envelope	69
Print labels	70
Change where files save by default	71
Personalise the Quick Access Toolbar	72
Learn more	74

Introduction

After you've created documents you'll probably want to share them. You can share in all kinds of ways, and almost all sharing tasks are achieved from the File tab, with which you're already familiar. You can use these sharing options to communicate the old-fashioned way by printing and posting (or faxing) letters and documents, or you can opt to communicate by sending a document via email. If you're looking to send a CV or something else electronically, but in a more professional way, you can even save and send the file as a PDF (Portable Document Format), among other options.

You can also personalise Word to better suit your needs. You can change where files save by default and customise the Quick Access Toolbar, for instance. Word offers these and plenty of other options for personalisation.

Email a document

Unless you're specifically asked to mail or fax a document, or if you've printed a Get Well or Sympathy card (or something similar), for the most part, email is an appropriate way to share a document with someone else. Your children would likely rather receive email, as would your employers or employees. Some book agents and publishers would rather receive chapters in an email than in the post!

1 In Word, with a document to email open, click the File tab.

2 Click Save & Send.

3 Click Send Using E-mail.

4 Click Send as Attachment.

? DID YOU KNOW?

When you send a document as an attachment, a copy is sent and the original remains on your computer.

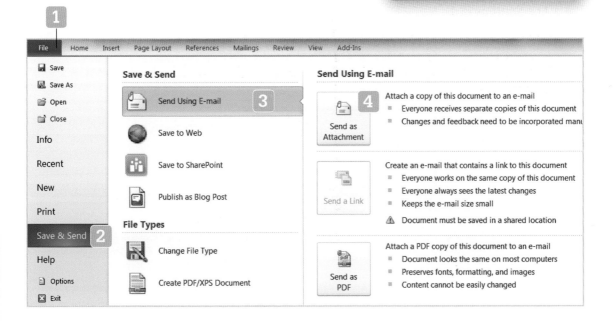

? DID YOU KNOW?

If you use a specific font in a document and email it as an attachment to someone who does not have the font you used, a different font will be substituted by their computer.

HOT TIP: If you don't want the recipients of the attachment to be able to easily edit it and/or you want to preserve fonts and images, send as a PDF or XPS.

Save and send a document as a PDF

Sending a document as a PDF is an acceptable way to send a file while preserving fonts, images, and reducing the recipient's ability to change or edit the file. You should send CVs as PDFs, as well as invoices, contracts, budgets, expenses reports, estimates, and similar sensitive items that you do not want altered, or documents that are in their final form and ready for the printer, such as brochures or playbills.

1 In Word, with a document to email open, click the File tab.

2 Click Save & Send.

3 Click Send Using E-mail.

4 Click Send as PDF.

5 Complete the email and click Send.

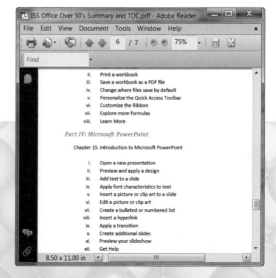

? DID YOU KNOW?

PDF files open in Adobe Reader 9 or a variation of it, as shown here.

Print a document

Sometimes you just want to print a document and put it in the post or head to the supermarket. Printing is easy in Word.

1 In Word, with a document to print open, click the File tab.

2 Click Print.

3 To create a simple print, click Print.

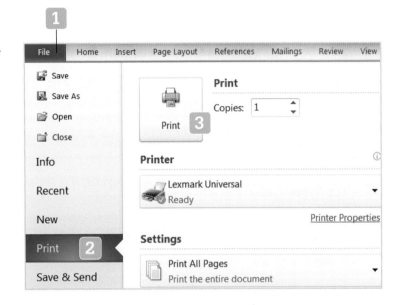

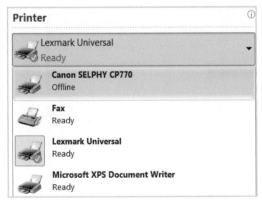

HOT TIP: Note the other options available, including the options to change the paper size, to print only specific pages, and to change the print margins.

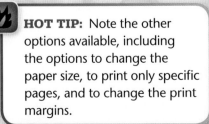

DID YOU KNOW?
Click the arrow next to the default printer to see other printers that may be available. If a printer is unavailable, it'll appear "offline".

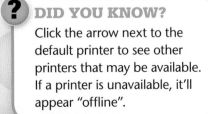

Explore printer settings

If you only occasionally print ordinary text documents, printer settings may not be of any importance to you. If you print a lot, you may be concerned with using less ink, using a specific type or size of paper, changing the page orientation from Portrait to Landscape, and more. You do this from the Printer Settings options.

1 Click File, and click Print.

2 Select your printer from the Print options page.

3 Click Printer Properties.

Printer ⓘ

Lexmark Universal **2**
Ready

3 Printer Properties

4 Because printers vary, printer options will also vary. Work through the tabs to see the options, selecting them as desired.

5 To save ink, lower the resolution settings or, if a slider is available, move it left to apply less ink.

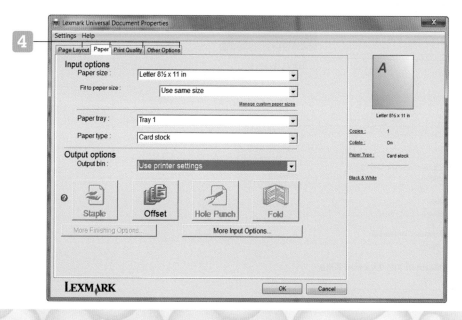

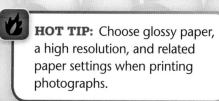

HOT TIP: Choose glossy paper, a high resolution, and related paper settings when printing photographs.

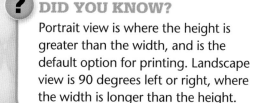

DID YOU KNOW?

Portrait view is where the height is greater than the width, and is the default option for printing. Landscape view is 90 degrees left or right, where the width is longer than the height.

Print an envelope

There are two ways to print an envelope. You can use a template from the File tab, from the New options, and replace the placeholders with your own data, or you can use the Envelopes and Labels dialog box in Word 2010. Try both and see which one works best for you. Here, we'll print an envelope using the latter option.

1 Open a new document in Word.

2 Click the Mailings tab.

3 In the Create group on the far left side, click Envelopes.

4 Type the required information.

5 Click Options.

6 Choose the desired envelope size.

7 Click OK, and click Print.

8 Load the envelope as required by your printer or perform other printer-related steps.

? DID YOU KNOW?
Some data may be populated automatically if the address is already included in a document you have open and are working on.

🔥 HOT TIP: When working from a template, select the placeholder data and type over it with your own data.

Print labels

As with envelopes, you can print labels from the Mailings tab or from a template. Either is fine, but the templates offer information on what type of label to use for best results, which makes printing labels practically foolproof.

1 Click File, and click New.

2 Click Labels and browse until you find the label you want to print.

3 Replace the boilerplate text with your own.

4 Click File and Print, making sure to insert the proper label paper into the printer.

5 Configure any other printer properties as applicable.

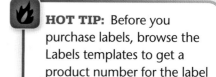

HOT TIP: Before you purchase labels, browse the Labels templates to get a product number for the label you'd like to use.

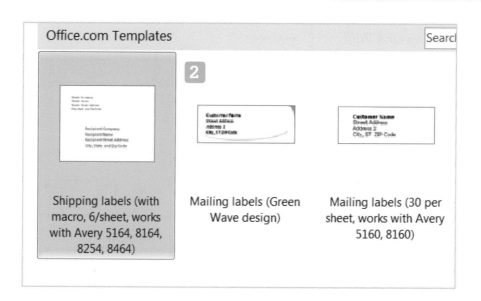

Office.com Templates   Searc

2

Shipping labels (with macro, 6/sheet, works with Avery 5164, 8164, 8254, 8464)

Mailing labels (Green Wave design)

Mailing labels (30 per sheet, works with Avery 5160, 8160)

HOT TIP: Use Copy and Paste when creating labels instead of retyping the information.

 DID YOU KNOW?
You can insert and resize clip art to fit in a label, such as your company logo or the flag of your country.

Change where files save by default

When you click File and then Save, Word automatically points you to the folder it thinks is the best place for you to save your files. In Windows 7, that's your Documents folder. You may want to save in a different folder most of the time, though, and if that's the case you can tell Microsoft Word where that folder is, and offer that folder as the default instead of Documents.

1 Click File, and click Options.

2 Click Save and for Default file location, click Browse.

3 Browse to the folder, click OK, and click OK again.

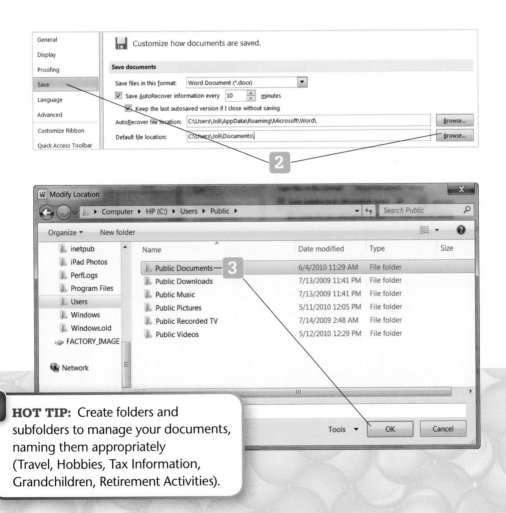

HOT TIP: Create folders and subfolders to manage your documents, naming them appropriately (Travel, Hobbies, Tax Information, Grandchildren, Retirement Activities).

Personalise the Quick Access Toolbar

The Quick Access Toolbar is the small toolbar that appears below the Ribbon. It contains Save, Undo Typing, and Redo Typing. You can add commands there you use often, and we suggest Open Recent File, E-mail, Print Preview and Print, and Quick Print.

1. Click the down arrow on the Quick Access Toolbar.

2. Click any command to add.

3. To add a command that isn't shown, click More Commands.

DID YOU KNOW?

You can move the Quick Access Toolbar so that it's above the Ribbon, if desired.

4 From the resulting dialog box, select any command in the left pane and click Add to add it to the Quick Access Toolbar. Here we're adding Format Painter.

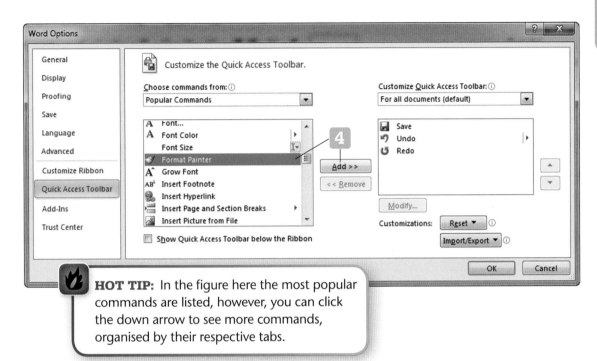

HOT TIP: In the figure here the most popular commands are listed, however, you can click the down arrow to see more commands, organised by their respective tabs.

HOT TIP: If the icons on the Quick Access Toolbar (or the Ribbon) are too small for you to see easily, change the display settings for your entire computer in Control Panel. Ours is set to 125%, which makes everything just a little bit larger.

Learn more

Obviously we can't introduce everything about Word in only a few chapters; we'd need an entire chapter to briefly introduce macros, for instance. A macro offers a way to create a shortcut for a task you perform repeatedly and requires you to 'record' the steps you use to complete the task. After it's recorded, you can have it perform the task with a single click of the mouse. But you can learn more easily; just click the blue question mark in the top right corner of Word. You'll find Help files, tutorials, and more.

1️⃣ Click the blue question mark in the top right corner.

2️⃣ Browse the available files and, then, type a keyword into the Search window.

3️⃣ Now, open Internet Explorer and visit http://office.microsoft.com.

4️⃣ Browse this web site, noting there are lots of tabs to explore, including Clip Art and Downloads.

5️⃣ Click Help and How-to.

6️⃣ Choose any product to learn more, get help from other users, and access tutorials.

ALERT: "Googling" for solutions to problems won't always offer solutions that work. If you have a problem or need help, look to Microsoft first.

HOT TIP: Make sure you're connected to the internet when you access the Help files. You'll want to be able to access the files stored at Office.com.

5 Introduction to Microsoft Outlook

Get a free email address	77
Start Outlook the first time and input email information	78
Input a secondary email account	80
Set one account as the default account	81
Check for new emails	82
Stay in Mail view	83
Read (and delete) an email	84
Add a sender to the address book	85
Change how often Outlook checks for emails	87
Reply to or forward an email	88
Compose a new email	89
Explore advanced formatting options	91
Attach a file	92
Insert a picture	93
Edit a picture	95
Request receipts	97
Preview an attachment	98
Open and save attachments	99
Use Zoom	100
Keep your Inbox clean	101
Empty Sent and Deleted Items folders	102
Create folders	103
Move mail into folders	105

Introduction

Microsoft Outlook is the email management program included with various editions of Microsoft Office 2010. You use Outlook to send and receive emails, maintain a calendar, manage contacts, keep notes and create tasks, and manage email you want to keep, among other things. Outlook is not included in the Home and Student edition of Microsoft Office, but you can purchase it separately if you decide you want it.

In this chapter you'll learn how to get started with Microsoft Outlook, including inputting email account information, reading and responding to emails, formatting emails and inserting pictures, and similar "introductory" tasks. In later chapters you'll learn about other features such as the Calendar and Contacts.

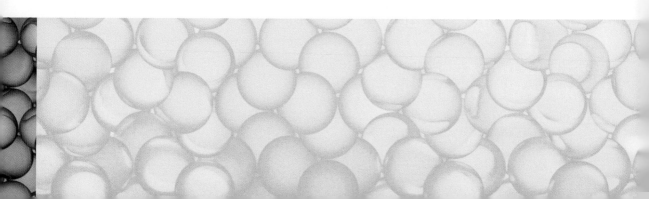

Get a free email address

If you don't have an email address, you can get one for free, and quite easily. Even if you already have an email address you might want another. You can use a web-based email address from an entity like Microsoft to communicate with public companies and web sites to make purchases, shop, sign in, and even make travel reservations, all the while keeping your personal email address private.

1 Visit www.live.com.

2 Click Sign up.

3 Fill in the required information and click I accept at the bottom of the page.

4 Note that when you get a new Live email address you also get a free, customised, web page, just for you. Explore and personalise this page as desired.

? DID YOU KNOW?

From your new Live home page, you'll have access to SkyDrive. You can use this feature to upload files from your computer to a web server in "the cloud". You can store files there to back them up, access them from another computer (like the one at your child's house), or share them.

HOT TIP: If you're creating an email account for logging in to web sites to chat or share ideas, consider creating an email address that does not include your actual name. Instead, opt for something like NewsJunkie65@live.com or GrandmalovesJr@live.com to maintain your privacy.

HOT TIP: Get a free email address from Microsoft to use publicly, and reduce the number of people who know your "real" email address to reduce (or avoid more) spam.

Start Outlook the first time and input email information

You may currently get your mail from a web page on the internet or with an email program like Outlook Express, Mail, or Windows Live Mail. You may also use an older version of Outlook. No matter what you use, when you start Outlook for the first time, you'll be asked to set it up and input information regarding your email account(s).

1 Open Microsoft Outlook.

2 When prompted to create an email account, verify Yes is selected and click Next.

3 If prompted regarding the type of account to create, choose E-mail account and click Next.

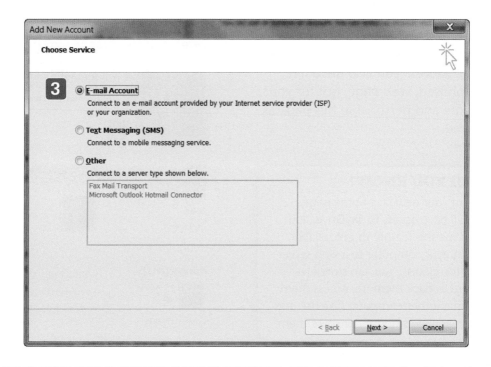

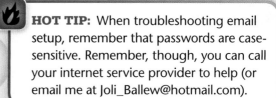

HOT TIP: If you did not create a shortcut to Outlook as detailed in Chapter 1, you'll have to click Start, All Programs, Microsoft Office, and then Microsoft Outlook 2010 to open it.

HOT TIP: When troubleshooting email setup, remember that passwords are case-sensitive. Remember, though, you can call your internet service provider to help (or email me at Joli_Ballew@hotmail.com).

4 Input the required information including your display name (this can be anything), your email address, and your password.

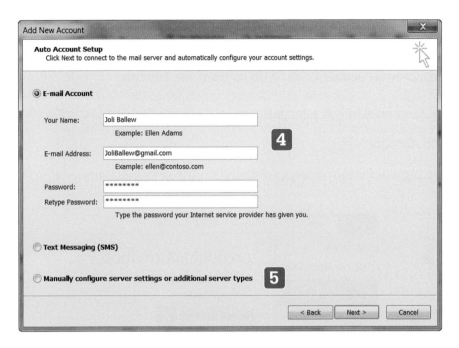

5 Wait to see if Outlook can configure the email account on its own. If it cannot, select Manually configure server settings or additional server types.

6 If you have to manually configure settings, call your ISP (internet service provider) for the information to input. Input the information, and click Next.

7 Click Close and Finish when the information has been successfully entered.

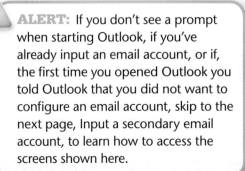

ALERT: If you don't see a prompt when starting Outlook, if you've already input an email account, or if, the first time you opened Outlook you told Outlook that you did not want to configure an email account, skip to the next page, Input a secondary email account, to learn how to access the screens shown here.

HOT TIP: You may be prompted to upgrade account settings Outlook 2003 or 2007 if you've used those programs in the past. Follow the prompts to do that if so.

Input a secondary email account

If you aren't prompted to create an email address when Outlook starts, or if you want to add a second email account, you'll do so from the File tab.

1 Click File, and note Info is selected.

2 Click Add Account.

3 Fill in the required information as detailed on the previous page.

DID YOU KNOW?
Email is short for electronic mail.

ALERT: If you're using an older Hotmail account from Microsoft, you'll need to install the Windows Live Hotmail Connector, available free at www.microsoft.com/downloads.

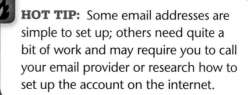
HOT TIP: Some email addresses are simple to set up; others need quite a bit of work and may require you to call your email provider or research how to set up the account on the internet.

Set one account as the default account

If you set up more than one email account, the first account you set up is the default account. The default account is used unless you specifically state otherwise. You can change which account is the default account from Account Settings.

1 In Outlook, click the File tab.

2 Click Account Settings, and Account Settings.

3 Click the account to set as the default.

4 Click Set as Default.

5 Click Close.

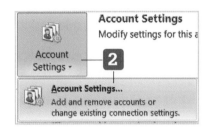

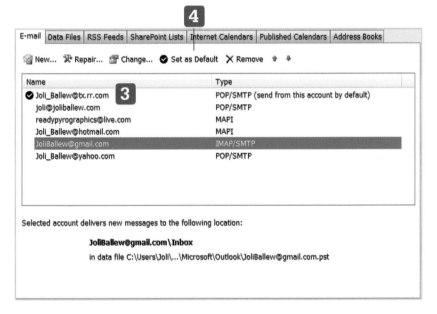

HOT TIP: If you right-click a picture of your grandchildren, and click Send To:, then Email Recipient, the email will automatically be configured to send from your default email address.

? DID YOU KNOW? Click any account and click Repair to make changes to the account.

HOT TIP: You can click any account and click Delete to remove it.

Check for new emails

Outlook checks for new emails every 30 minutes, but you can check for email any time by clicking Send/Receive All Folders from the Home tab. If you're waiting for a quick response to a question, like "What was my total cholesterol level?", or "Where will we meet for lunch?", check email manually as desired.

1 In Outlook, click the Home tab.

2 Verify Inbox is selected in the left pane.

3 Click Send/Receive All Folders.

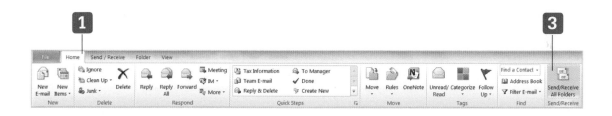

> **? DID YOU KNOW?**
>
> You can categorise any message with a colour code. You may want to categorise important messages with red, messages that pertain to your garden club with green, and messages from airlines or travel agents blue. Click Categorize from the Home tab to select a colour to apply to any selected email.

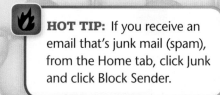 **HOT TIP:** If you receive an email that's junk mail (spam), from the Home tab, click Junk and click Block Sender.

> **? DID YOU KNOW?**
>
> You can access Send/Receive All Folders from the Send/Receive tab and from the Quick Access Toolbar (that runs across the top of the Outlook window).

Stay in Mail view

Outlook offers various views. In this chapter you need to be in Mail view. There's also a Calendar view, Contacts view, Tasks view, Notes view, Folder view, and Shortcuts view. If you're ever unable to locate the commands outlined in this chapter, make sure you're in Mail view.

1 In the left pane of Outlook, note there are options for moving from view to view:

- Click Mail in the long list that may appear.
- Click Mail in a shorter list that may appear.
- Click Mail in the thumbnail list that may appear.

2 You can change the views by dragging from the top bar that runs across the Mail entry in the first and second figure, or the top bar shown in the third.

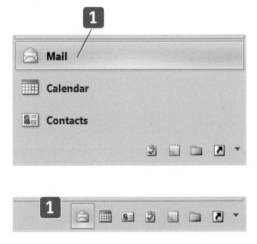

! ALERT: If at any time you do not see your Inbox, click any Mail icon shown in the three figures here and click Inbox.

? DID YOU KNOW?
Folder view offers Inbox and other mail folders, as well as Calendar, Tasks, and other features in the left pane.

Read (and delete) an email

If you're anxious to receive an email, you can always write one from yourself to yourself. You can email me at joli_ballew@hotmail.com and I'll send a reply too. However you go about getting an email in your Inbox, though, you simply click it to read it.

1 Check for new email as detailed on the previous page.

2 Click any email once to open it.

3 Read the contents of the email in the Reading Pane.

4 Click Delete to delete the email after reading it.

HOT TIP: Here the Reading Pane is shown across the bottom of the page, but it can also appear to the right.

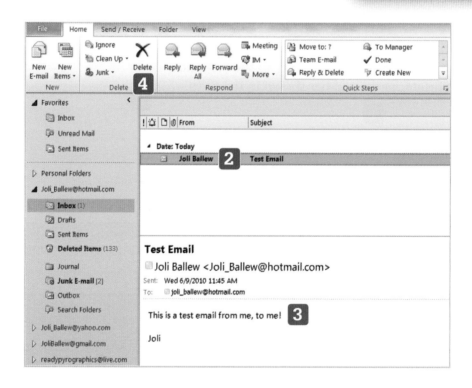

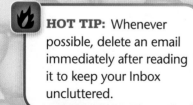

HOT TIP: Whenever possible, delete an email immediately after reading it to keep your Inbox uncluttered.

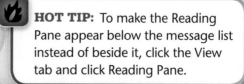

HOT TIP: To make the Reading Pane appear below the message list instead of beside it, click the View tab and click Reading Pane.

Add a sender to the address book

Your email addresses are stored in Outlook's Address Book. You can access your address book from the Home tab. Although there are several ways to get email addresses into the address book, adding them from an email you receive is the easiest.

1 After you receive an email, click it to select it.

2 In the Reading Pane, locate the sender's email address.

3 Right-click the address.

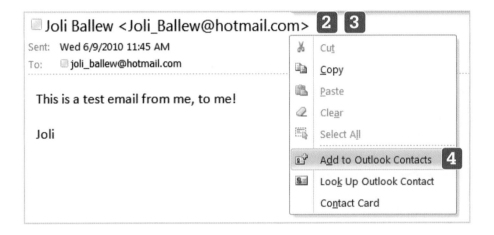

4 Click Add to Outlook Contacts.

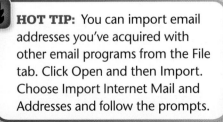

HOT TIP: You can import email addresses you've acquired with other email programs from the File tab. Click Open and then Import. Choose Import Internet Mail and Addresses and follow the prompts.

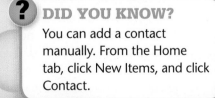

DID YOU KNOW?

You can add a contact manually. From the Home tab, click New Items, and click Contact.

5 Notice all of the available options for personalising the contacts, including the tabs. Type the desired information.

6 Click Save & Close.

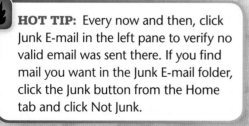

Change how often Outlook checks for emails

Even though your children and grandchildren know you are busy and are involved in lots of activities, they still expect you to read and respond to emails immediately. This is especially true if they think (or know) you are online or at your desk.

1 Click the File tab.

2 Click Options.

3 Click Advanced and scroll to access Send/Receive (if necessary).

? DID YOU KNOW?

Outlook comes preconfigured to check for emails every 30 minutes. You may want to change that to 5 or 10 minutes if your children are complaining you don't write back quickly enough.

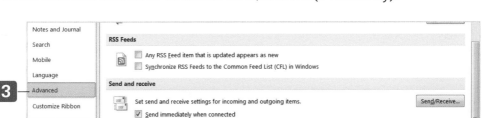

4 Click Send/Receive and change how often to check for new mail. Here it's set to 5 minutes.

5 Click Close and then, OK.

? DID YOU KNOW?

Chatting is quicker than sending emails and is better for short online conversations. Ask your children and grandchildren what messaging program they use and get it. Then, you can converse with them more easily when you're online. (We prefer the free Windows Live Messenger, from Microsoft's Windows Live suite.)

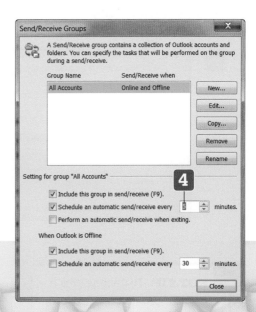

! ALERT: If you have a program like Windows Live Messenger set to log you in automatically when you boot your computer, your contacts will know when you are connected to the internet. Don't lie and say you weren't online; they'll know!

Reply to or forward an email

You can reply to or forward an email after reading it by clicking the Reply, Forward, or Reply All buttons. When you click Reply, your response is only sent to the person sending the email; when you click Reply All, a response is sent to the sender and everyone else included in the To or CC lines. When you click Forward, you get to select who the message should go to.

1 After reading an email, click Reply, Reply All, or Forward.

2 Compose your response.

3 If required, type recipient's email address.

4 If desired, format the text. Note that you can format text using the same tools as you can in Microsoft Word, including Bold, Italic, Underline, and more.

5 Click Send.

> ▶ **SEE ALSO:** For more information on CC, BCC, and other terms, refer to Compose a new email, right.

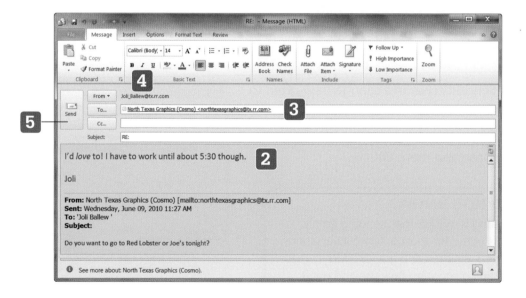

HOT TIP: To change which email account you send from, click the From button. In this figure, it's beside the email address shown (the default), joli_ballew@tx.rr.com.

? DID YOU KNOW?
You can apply colour to the entire email from the Options tab, under Page Color, or a theme from Themes.

Compose a new email

When you are ready to correspond with others via email, you compose a new email. During composition you can add a background colour, a theme, format text, use Cut, Copy, and Paste, and more.

1 In Outlook, from the Home tab, click New E-mail.

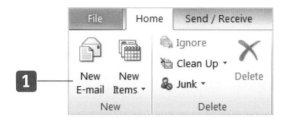

2 Type the recipient's email addresses in the To: line, or click To:, and then:
- In the Address Book list, double-click the name to add.
- Repeat to add additional names.
- Click OK.

 **DID YOU KNOW?**
To hide or show the BCC line in any reply, forward, or new email, click the Options tab and click BCC.

 SEE ALSO: Explore advanced formatting options, next.

3 Click next to Subject and type a meaningful and representative subject title.

4 Click inside the body and type your message, noting that you can opt to format your email any way you like, as shown here.

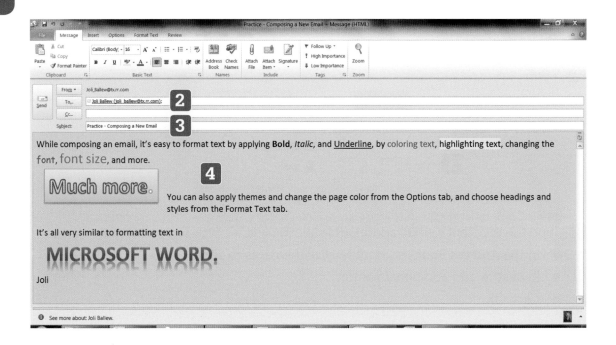

Explore advanced formatting options

While composing, replying to, or forwarding an email, you have access to several formatting options, many of which were outlined in the chapters on Microsoft Word.

1 While composing an email and while typing inside the body of an email, click the Insert tab. Then:

- Click Horizontal Line.
- Click Symbol and click any symbol in the list to add it.
- Select the first letter in the email body, and click Drop Cap.

2 Click the Options tab. Then:

- Click Themes, and select any theme.
- Click Page Color and select any page colour.

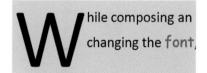

3 Click the Insert tab again and then:

- Click WordArt.
- Select a WordArt type.
- Type a word.

4 Complete the email and click Send.

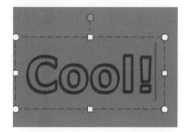

▶ SEE ALSO: Chapter 3: Use Find and Replace; Use the Format Painter; Select and replace text.

? DID YOU KNOW?

While composing an email, you can insert clip art from the Insert tab. Click Clip Art. See chapter 2 for more information.

Attach a file

You can attach files to an email so they will be sent with it. You can attach almost anything, from a sales brochure to a budget spreadsheet; from a slide presentation to a video montage. If the files you want to send aren't incredibly large, you can also send a song you want someone to learn or a video of your 60th birthday party.

1 Compose a new email or reply to or forward one.

2 Click the Insert tab.

3 Click Attach File.

4 Locate the file to attach, click it once, and click Insert.

5 Complete the email as desired, and click Send.

? **DID YOU KNOW?**

When the recipient receives an email that contains an attachment, it'll look like a paperclip on the email.

? **DID YOU KNOW?**

Click Attach Item to attach an item from Outlook, such as another email, a contact card, a Calendar event, and more.

Insert a picture

Although you can attach pictures you can also insert pictures directly into the body of an email. Inserting pictures is a good idea when you want to add information about each picture before or after it, or if you want to include pictures in a specific order. When you insert a picture the recipient can almost always view the picture inside the email too, reducing the need to open attached files.

1 While composing an email, click the Insert tab.

2 Click Picture.

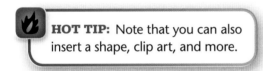
HOT TIP: Note that you can also insert a shape, clip art, and more.

3 Browse to the picture to insert and double-click it.

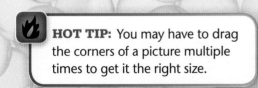
HOT TIP: You may have to drag the corners of a picture multiple times to get it the right size.

? DID YOU KNOW?
You can drag and drop a picture inside the body of an email to reposition it.

4 Resize the picture by dragging from the corners.

5 Repeat as desired to add more pictures.

6 Leave this email open and continue to the next section.

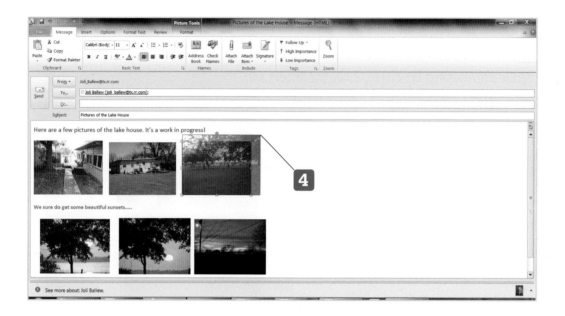

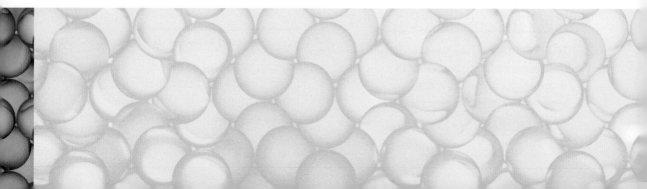

Edit a picture

With a picture inserted and selected, the Picture Tools tab becomes available. There you can edit the picture.

1 Select any picture and click the new Picture Tools tab.

2 Use the tools to edit your pictures:

- Click Corrections to sharpen, soften, or change the brightness or contrast of a picture.
- Click Color to change the intensity.
- Click Artistic Effects to add effects such as watercolour.
- Click any option in the Pictures Styles group to apply it.
- Click any Picture Border option to apply it.

3 Continue experimenting as desired.

HOT TIP: To rotate a picture, select it and drag from the top middle point.

? DID YOU KNOW?

The Picture Tools tab will only appear after you've inserted a picture and selected it; to hide the tab click outside any picture.

Request receipts

When you need to send something important via email, such as a receipt, invoice, estimate, formal request, formal response, complaint, and the like, request a read and/or delivery receipt before sending. A delivery receipt will let you know the email has arrived at its destination; a read receipt will let you know the recipient has opened the email.

1 After composing a new email and prior to sending it, click the Options tab.

2 Click Request a Delivery Receipt if desired.

3 Click Request a Read Receipt if desired.

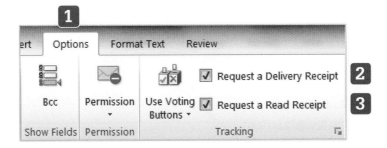

? **DID YOU KNOW?**
A delivery receipt is also appropriate if you are concerned the size of the attachment you're sending is too large for the recipient's mail box. (Some service providers impose limits on file size while others do not.)

! **ALERT:** Just because an email has been opened does not necessarily mean it's been read.

! **ALERT:** Some people turn off the option to send read receipts, so even if you ask for one you may not get one. A delivery receipt is sent by the email service, though, and will likely be sent. (You'll be notified if a delivery receipt was unable to be sent, but you will not be notified if the recipient declines to send a read receipt.)

Preview an attachment

When you receive an email that contains an attachment, you can often preview the attachment before opening it.

1 Select the email that contains the attachment. In the Reading Pane, notice Message is selected. The attachment is beside it.

2 Click the name of the attachment, in this case Resume 2010.doc.

3 Notice that you can preview the attachment in the Reading Pane without opening the attachment.

4 Click Message again to return to the message.

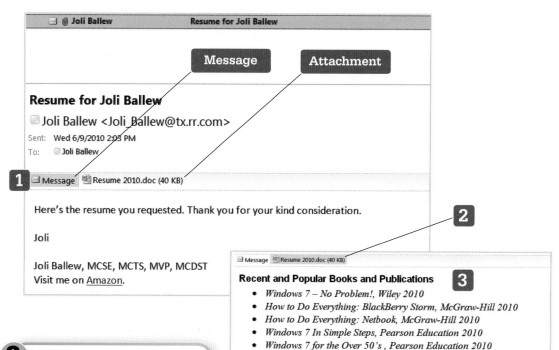

? DID YOU KNOW?

Not all attachments can be previewed, only those that are supported in Outlook and for which you have a reader installed. For the most part this includes any Microsoft document and most pictures.

! ALERT: Never open any attachment that you aren't expecting. When in doubt, email the sender and ask what the attachment contains and if it's safe to open. Banks, insurance companies, doctors, and the like rarely send attachments.

Open and save attachments

To open an attachment that cannot be previewed, an attachment you want to view in full screen, or an attachment you want to edit, double-click it. It will open in its related program (documents open in Microsoft Word; presentations open in Microsoft PowerPoint). Once open you can save the attachment using the features in the program, generally an option from the File tab.

You can also save an attachment without opening it.

1 Right-click the attachment name and click Save As.

2 Browse to the location to save the file.

3 Name the file and click Save.

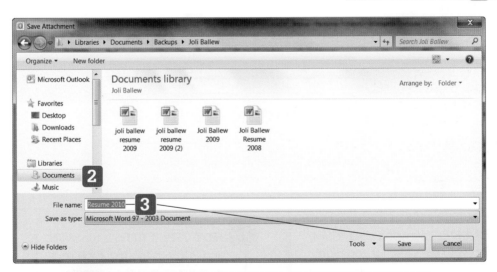

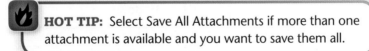

HOT TIP: Select Save All Attachments if more than one attachment is available and you want to save them all.

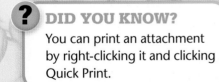

? DID YOU KNOW?

You can print an attachment by right-clicking it and clicking Quick Print.

Use Zoom

Our eyes aren't what they used to be! If you're having trouble reading an email in the Reading Pane, you can use the Zoom slider to increase the size of the words and pictures.

1 Select an email and view it in the Reading Pane.

2 Use the slider to zoom in on the body of the email.

3 To zoom in another way:
- Double-click the email to open it in a new window.
- Click Zoom.
- Click 200%.
- Click OK.

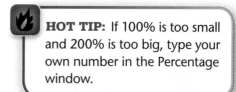

ALERT: You won't always have access to the slider for zooming, such as when you are previewing attachments.

HOT TIP: If 100% is too small and 200% is too big, type your own number in the Percentage window.

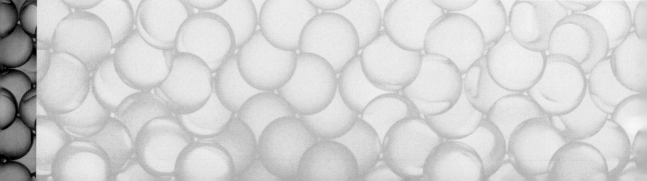

Keep your Inbox clean

The fewer emails you have in your Inbox, the better. The only emails that should be in your Inbox are those that need attention and any you haven't had time to read or reply to. For instance, you may have a flyer for the community centre to edit, a gardening question from a friend you've yet to find an answer to, or an estimate for a repair you'd like to compare to others you're expecting.

Take a look at your Inbox and ask yourself the following questions.

- Can I delete this email? Have I dealt with it appropriately?
- Is this a receipt, estimate, or invoice I need to print and permanently file? If so, can I delete it once I've done that?
- Is this email really so funny or interesting that I can't delete it?
- If I can't delete the email now, when can I? What do I need to do before I can delete it?
- If I were to create folders in Outlook to manage the email I want to keep, what would the names of those folders be? (Tax, Doctors, Insurance Information, Boating, Travel, Languages, Work, etc.)

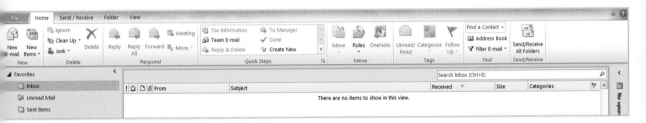

HOT TIP: A clean Inbox signifies you've dealt with all of your email, or at least, are successfully managing it. If it can't be empty though, try to keep it under 20 items.

HOT TIP: Although we all want to be "green" and watch how much paper we use, and we'd like to save money by not printing anything unnecessarily, it's wise to print important documents you receive in an email and file them (in case something happens to your computer).

? DID YOU KNOW?
You can create folders in Outlook that you can later move email into. This will help you maintain a clean Inbox while at the same time allowing you to keep emails you deem important.

Empty Sent and Deleted Items folders

Email collects in the corners and crevices of Outlook in places you might not expect, similar to how cobwebs collect in doorways and corners when you're not looking. There are two main hiding places for emails; all emails you send are saved in the Sent Items folder, and all emails you delete are saved in the Deleted Items folder. After a year or so, you can imagine how this would build up!

1 Locate the Sent Items folder in Outlook. You may have multiple Sent Items folders if you have multiple email addresses configured.

2 Right-click this folder and click Delete All to delete every item in the folder.

3 Right-click the Deleted Items folder.

4 Click Empty Folder.

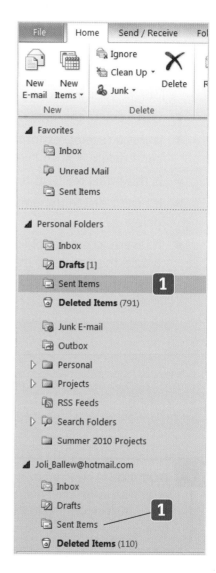

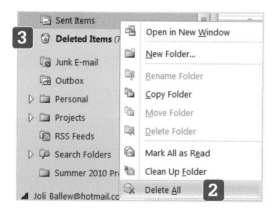

HOT TIP: If you want to keep, say, the last month of sent emails, in the Sent Items folder, select the emails to delete and click Delete from the Home tab. Note that you can select multiple, contiguous emails by holding down the Shift key while selecting. (You can do the same thing with the Deleted Items folder.)

HOT TIP: We think it's best to keep about 3 months of Sent and Deleted Items, just in case you need to access them again.

Create folders

We understand that you can't delete everything in your Inbox and that there are some things you do need to keep. To keep order, though, create email folders for those items and move them into the new folders regularly.

1 Click Personal Folders. This is the "Outlook Today" view.

2 Right-click Personal Folders and click New Folder.

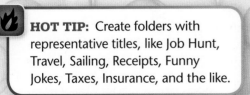

HOT TIP: Create folders with representative titles, like Job Hunt, Travel, Sailing, Receipts, Funny Jokes, Taxes, Insurance, and the like.

3 Type a name for the folder.

4 Decide where to create the folder. The folder you create will appear underneath the item you select.

5 Click OK.

6 Note the new folder in the left pane of Outlook.

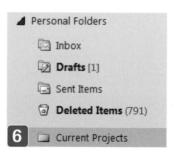

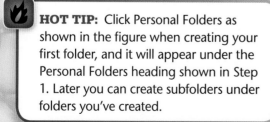

HOT TIP: Click Personal Folders as shown in the figure when creating your first folder, and it will appear under the Personal Folders heading shown in Step 1. Later you can create subfolders under folders you've created.

? DID YOU KNOW?

If you create folders in Outlook and then sync (synchronise) your computer with a device like an iPad, those folders will be copied to the device during your first sync.

Move mail into folders

Now that you've created folders it's easy to move emails into them. You simply drag an email from its current folder to the appropriate folder.

1 Select the email to move.

2 While holding down the left mouse button, drag the email to the folder you want to move it to.

3 Let go to drop it in the folder.

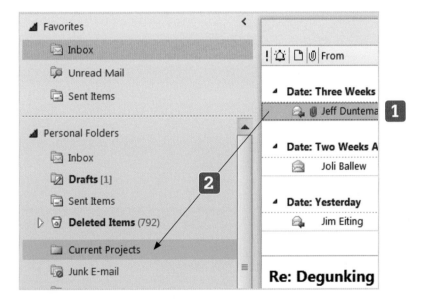

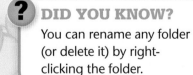 **HOT TIP:** You can drag emails from any folder to any folder. (Even from Deleted Items to your Inbox!)

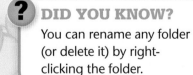 **? DID YOU KNOW?** You can rename any folder (or delete it) by right-clicking the folder.

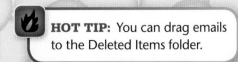 **HOT TIP:** You can drag emails to the Deleted Items folder.

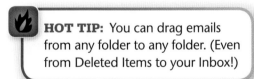

6 Explore Calendar and contacts

Explore Calendar view   109

Add an appointment   110

Set a reminder   112

Explore Folder List view   113

Browse contacts   114

Add a contact   115

Add a contact from an email   117

Create a contact group   118

Introduction

Outlook offers much more than a way to manage your emails. It comes with a calendar, a way to manage contacts and more (like options for creating tasks and notes). The Calendar enables you to create appointments, create events and set reminders so you won't forget about them. The Contacts feature enables you to keep detailed information about all of the contacts you have, even if you do not communicate with them using your computer. You already know how to switch between views, but, to be on the safe side, we'll start out with that task to review it.

Explore Calendar view

At the bottom of the left pane, you'll see an icon that looks like a calendar. It will likely be in one of the forms shown here. Click a Calendar option to get to Calendar view. (You have to click the Mail icon to return to Mail view.)

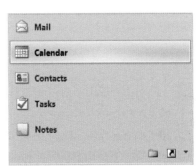

1 Click the Calendar icon to access Calendar view.

2 Verify which calendar is selected, in this case, Calendar.

3 From the Home tab, click Day, Work Week, Week, and Month to explore the views.

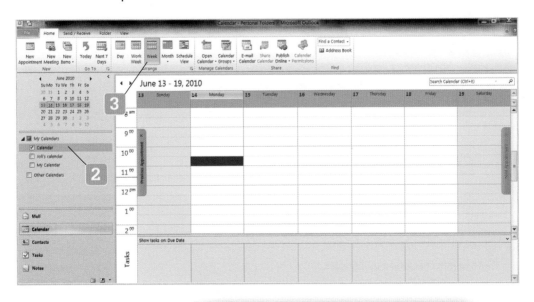

► SEE ALSO: Explore Folder List view to have access to your calendar while also having access to your Inbox.

? DID YOU KNOW?
If you've worked with calendars before or have synced calendars you have already set up somewhere else (like Google.com or Live.com), you'll see the additional calendars here.

🔥 HOT TIP: When you use Outlook's Calendar feature to store and manage your day-to-day activities, events, appointments, and the like, each day when you open Outlook you can easily see (in the To-Do bar) what's in store for that day. This will allow you to focus on more important things, like your grandchildren or your tennis game!

Add an appointment

To fully utilise the calendar, you have to add appointments or events. You can also add birthdays, sports tournaments, or even a list of what you want to accomplish on a specific day. You input appointments and events by double-clicking any date (and/or time) on the calendar.

1 Double-click any time or date in any calendar.

2 From the Appointment tab, input the appropriate information:

- A subject in the Subject line.
- A location in the Location line.
- The start and end times. (Notice the arrows.)
- Notes regarding the appointment.

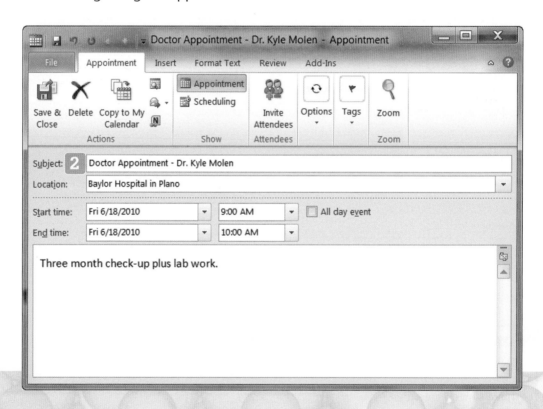

ALERT: If you click All day event, the Appointment tab changes to an Event tab and the start and end times become unavailable. Outlook considers an event an all-day commitment.

3 From the Appointment or Event tab, click Save & Close.

4 Note the new appointment or event is in the calendar.

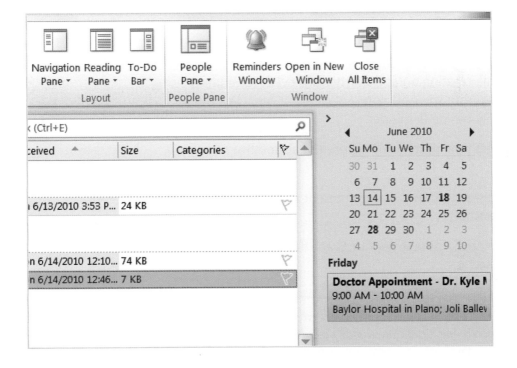

 HOT TIP: Double-click any appointment to edit it. (Just remember to click Save & Close when you've finished editing.)

! ALERT: You have to click the Mail icon to return to Mail view and see the appointment or event in the To-Do bar. (If you can't see the To-Do bar, click the View tab, click To-Do bar, and click Normal.)

Set a reminder

You can configure Outlook to remind you with a sound and pop-up box before an appointment or event. Consider entering events for birthdays and anniversaries, and then set a reminder for a few days prior. The option to create a reminder is available during appointment creation.

1 While creating an appointment or event (or editing one), from the Appointment or Event tab, click the arrow beside Reminder.

2 Select how much time before the appointment or event you'd like to be reminded of it.

3 If desired, make the appointment High or Low Importance.

4 From the Appointment or Event tab, click Save & Close.

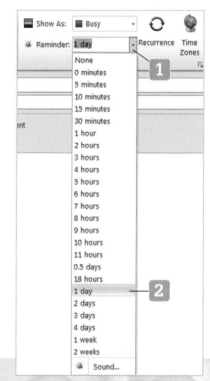

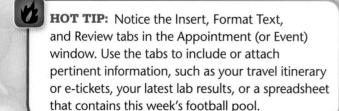

HOT TIP: If you want the event to recur, click Recurrence. Configure a yearly recurrence for birthdays, anniversaries, annual golf tournaments, and family reunions; configure weekly recurrences for exercise classes or seeing the children.

HOT TIP: Notice the Insert, Format Text, and Review tabs in the Appointment (or Event) window. Use the tabs to include or attach pertinent information, such as your travel itinerary or e-tickets, your latest lab results, or a spreadsheet that contains this week's football pool.

ALERT: If you can't see the Reminder option in Step 1, maximise the Appointment (or Event) window.

Explore Folder List view

You know about Calendar view and Mail view. You can likely surmise that clicking other icons will take you to other views. You're right! There's one interesting view, though, and that's Folder List view. With Folder List view you have access to your Inbox, Calendar, Tasks, and Notes, all from one window. You may prefer this view to all of the other views you've experienced so far.

1 In the Navigation pane, click the icon for Folder List view.

2 Note the subtle differences between this view and Mail view. Here you can access (among other things):

    a Inbox – To view and respond to new emails, to create new emails, and to attach files and pictures.

    b Calendar – To access your calendar, view, edit, and create appointments and events, email your calendar to others.

    c Notes – To view your notes, create new notes, share notes, and sort and filter notes.

    d Tasks – To view your tasks, create new tasks and task requests, and to sort and filter tasks.

> **Did you know?**
>
> Drag here to resize this pane.

ALERT: The features you'll have access to in Folder view for Mail, Calendar, Contacts, Tasks, and Notes are *limited* views and will not offer access to all of the features available for it. To access all features, click its icon to access the full view.

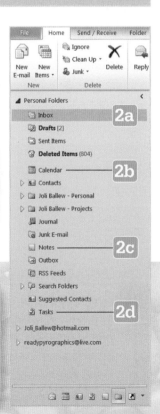

? DID YOU KNOW?

You can drag the separator line above the views shown here to change how the views are shown or listed.

? DID YOU KNOW?

Here, we've created our own folders to hold data we keep, including Joli Ballew – Personal and Joli Ballew – Projects. You may want to do the same.

Browse contacts

You can browse contacts to review information about them, edit the information, or share it. If you have trouble remembering information about a person, such as a spouse's name or children's names, what day of the week your gardener is supposed to mow your lawn, a friend's pet's name, or even their street address, add it. You can then easily access that information by browsing to the contact when you need it.

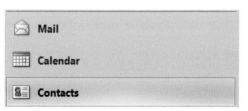

You can view your contacts in many ways:

- While in Contacts view, click any contact card to view it.
- While in Mail view, from the Home tab, click Address Book. (Note Find a contact, where you can type a contact's name to locate the Contact Card.)
- While composing a new email, click the To: button.
- From the Folder List view, by clicking Contacts.

 HOT TIP: When creating contacts add as much information as possible, including phone numbers, addresses, and other data. That data can be synced to devices capable of being synced with Outlook, such as the iPad.

 DID YOU KNOW?

If you have multiple email addresses you may also have multiple contact categories. Access all of these from Contact view.

Add a contact

You should try to actively add contacts and related information for all of the people you communicate with. Even if you don't have an email address, you can add a telephone number, web site, or fax number, and create a sort of digital Rolodex for yourself.

1 In any view, click New Items.

2 Click Contact.

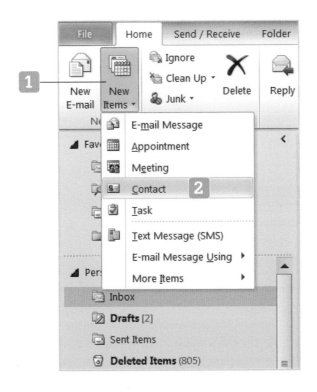

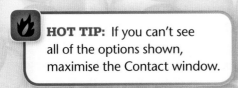

HOT TIP: If you can't see all of the options shown, maximise the Contact window.

3 Fill in as much as you like from the Contact tab.

4 Explore the other tabs, inputting information as desired.

5 When finished, click Save & Close.

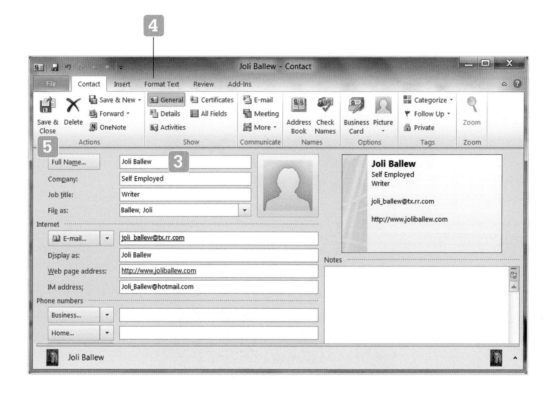

❓ DID YOU KNOW?

Click inside the Notes area and the options under the Insert tab will become available. You can then insert clip art, attach files or Outlook items, hyperlinks, and more.

Add a contact from an email

When you get an email from a person who is not yet a contact, you can add them easily. You can obtain email addresses in CC: lines as well as To: lines, which will enable you to obtain email addresses for people that are in mailing lists and groups to which you belong.

1 In your Inbox, select an email.

2 Right-click the contact name or the email address on the email in the Reading pane.

3 Click Add to Outlook Contacts.

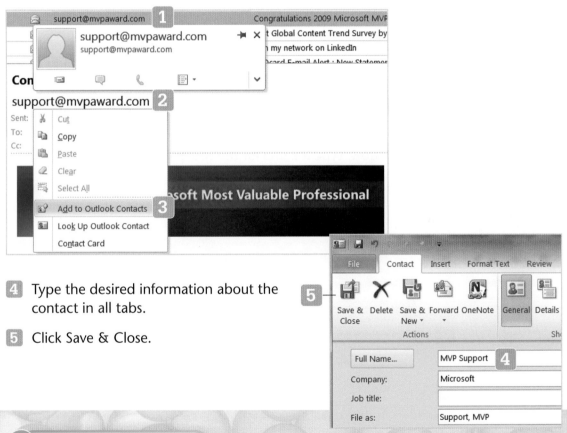

4 Type the desired information about the contact in all tabs.

5 Click Save & Close.

? DID YOU KNOW?
If the contact has already been added, you'll be prompted to edit or change the information.

! ALERT: Replying to an email does not add the contact to your contact list.

Create a contact group

When you have a group of people you communicate with often, you know how time-consuming it is to type all of their email addresses in the To: line or select them all from the Address Book. There's a better way. You can create a group and put their email addresses in it and, then, the next time you want to send an email to all of them, just type the group name in the To: line.

1 Click the Contacts icon in the Navigation pane to open Contacts view.

2 In Contacts view, from the Home tab, click New Contact Group.

3 In the Contact Group window, type a name for the group.

4 Click Add Members.

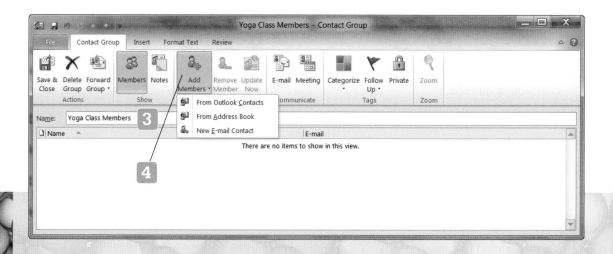

When prompted to choose from where to obtain the contacts, choose Outlook Contacts.

 Work through the list, double-clicking members to add. Click OK when finished.

7 With contacts added, click Save & Close.

HOT TIP: If you don't find the contacts you're looking for in Outlook Contacts, try another option, like Address Book.

HOT TIP: To send an email to everyone in the group, in the To: line of a new email, type the group name.

 DID YOU KNOW?

If, when sending an email to the group, you do not want to divulge your group's email addresses and contact names to everyone in the group, put the group name in the BCC: line of a new email. Put your own email address in the To: line.

7 Print, personalise, back up, and explore

Use Print Preview   123

Print an email   124

Print a calendar   126

Search for an email   127

Move the Quick Access Toolbar   129

Add Print to the Quick Access Toolbar   130

Add New E-mail to the Quick Access Toolbar   131

Add a custom group   133

Add your favourite commands to the custom group   135

Remove an item from the Ribbon   137

Understand the Outlook .pst file   138

Back up Outlook data   139

Export your address book   141

Archive messages   143

Learn more   144

Introduction

In this final chapter on Outlook, you'll learn how to search for emails you've "lost", and print emails you need to have in a hard copy. You'll personalise Outlook's interface, and back up your contacts, folders and email messages. You'll also learn where to go next to learn more.

While printing, backing up, and personalising are tasks you might expect to see in a final chapter on Outlook, you probably aren't aware of all of the options you actually have on the personalising front. You can remove tabs and tab groups from the Ribbon, and then add your own, populating them with your favourite commands. You can add icons to the Quick Access Toolbar, too, if your eyes are good enough to see them! No matter how you choose to apply what's here, though, all of it is about saving you time. So let's get started so you can get back to improving your golf game!

Use Print Preview

Print Preview allows you to see what an email will look like after you print it, without actually printing it. You may need to print dates and times for an event or a map with turn-by-turn directions. You may want to print a flyer to share it with a group or club. Who knows, you may even get some digital artwork from a grandchild you'd like to put on the fridge door!

1 In Outlook, click the File tab, and click Print.

2 Click Memo Style.

3 Verify the printer you want to use is selected.

4 If you need to zoom in on the preview, click it once. (Click again to zoom back out.)

5 Click the Home tab when finished.

> **? DID YOU KNOW?**
> All Office programs offer Print Preview, including Word, Excel, PowerPoint, and others.

> **🔥 HOT TIP:** If the Print Preview shows that the entire first page of an email you want to print contains the email addresses of other recipients, or that the last page is just a signature or picture, in Print Options, specify the pages you want to print (and thus, those you do not) prior to printing.

> **? DID YOU KNOW?**
> You can print from any folder, including Sent, Deleted, and even Junk E-Mail.

Print an email

You can print an email to share it with a friend or family member who does not have a computer or email address; you may want to print a funny joke, community event notice, or health alert. You can also print receipts you acquire from online shopping; dates, times, and directions for an event you plan to attend; or a document you receive, such as a CV, flyer, or property details.

1 Select the email to print.

2 Click the File tab and click Print.

3 Select the appropriate printer from the list, if more than one exists.

4 Click Print Options.

5 Configure the print options as desired.

6 Click Print.

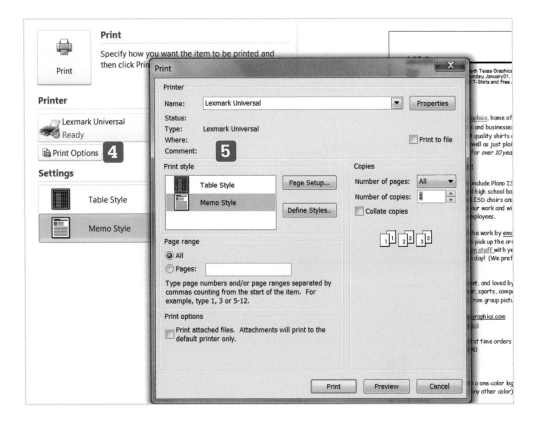

Print a calendar

One of the highlights of using Outlook's Calendar is that you can easily print calendar data in the most unique and surprising ways. The Tri-fold style is the perfect fit for a travel document case or passport holder, while the Calendar Details Style is best if you want the data to be printed as concisely as possible. There's even a Daily Style if you need to take today's entries with you and Monthly Style if you want to print your calendar and attach it to a community bulletin board.

1 Click the Calendar icon at the bottom of the Navigation pane to access Calendar view.

2 Select the appropriate calendar under My Calendars.

3 Click the File tab, and click Print.

4 Click each style option. Here, Weekly Agenda Style is selected.

5 Click Print Options if desired and configure additional settings.

6 Click Print.

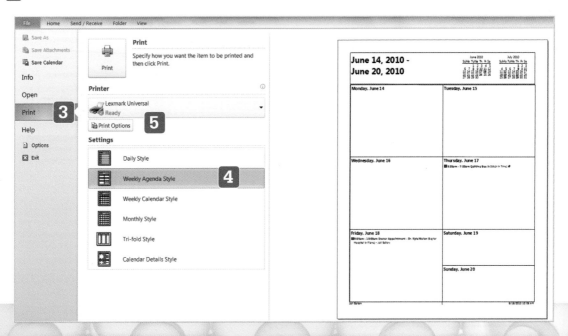

HOT TIP: When configuring print options, try Draft if it's available. You'll use less ink and save money too!

? DID YOU KNOW?

When printing a calendar you have the option to Hide details of private appointments. (You can denote an appointment as private when you create it.)

Search for an email

If you need to locate an email you've previously sent, deleted, moved to another folder, or otherwise "lost", you can locate it using the Search feature in Outlook. (It can't find your reading glasses though!) You only have to know a keyword associated with the email, perhaps the sender's name, group name, subject line, or a specific (and preferably unique) word that's in the body of the email.

1 In Outlook, locate the Search box.

2 Type a keyword.

3 If necessary, click Try searching again in All Mail Items.

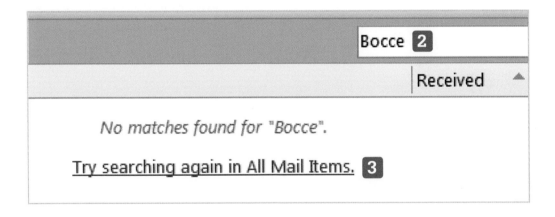

4 Click the item in the results to view it.

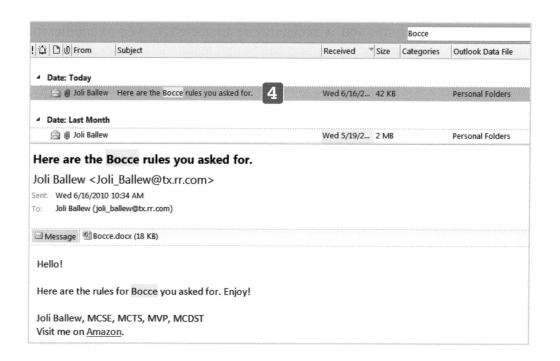

!	⌂	▯	◌	From	Subject	Received	▾	Size	Categories	Outlook Data File

▲ **Date: Today**

| 📨 ◌ Joli Ballew | Here are the Bocce rules you asked for. | **4** | Wed 6/16/2... | 42 KB | | Personal Folders |

▲ **Date: Last Month**

| 📨 ◌ Joli Ballew | | Wed 5/19/2... | 2 MB | | Personal Folders |

Here are the **Bocce** rules you asked for.

Joli Ballew <Joli_Ballew@tx.rr.com>

Sent: Wed 6/16/2010 10:34 AM

To: Joli Ballew (joli_ballew@tx.rr.com)

✉ Message   📄 Bocce.docx (18 KB)

Hello!

Here are the rules for **Bocce** you asked for. Enjoy!

Joli Ballew, MCSE, MCTS, MVP, MCDST
Visit me on Amazon.

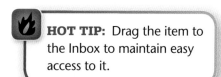

HOT TIP: Drag the item to the Inbox to maintain easy access to it.

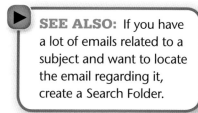

SEE ALSO: If you have a lot of emails related to a subject and want to locate the email regarding it, create a Search Folder.

Move the Quick Access Toolbar

The Quick Access Toolbar offers quick links to commands you use often: Send/Receive All Folders, Undo Typing, Redo Typing, Previous Item, and Next Item depending on the view and your current task. This toolbar can be a real timesaver if you configure it to meet your own, specific needs, and offers one-click access to commands you can hand-pick.

1 Click the arrow on the Quick Access Toolbar.

2 Click Show Below the Ribbon (or Show Above the Ribbon).

3 Note the new placement of the Quick Access Toolbar.

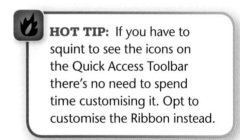

HOT TIP: If you have to squint to see the icons on the Quick Access Toolbar there's no need to spend time customising it. Opt to customise the Ribbon instead.

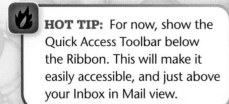

HOT TIP: For now, show the Quick Access Toolbar below the Ribbon. This will make it easily accessible, and just above your Inbox in Mail view.

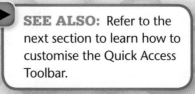

SEE ALSO: Refer to the next section to learn how to customise the Quick Access Toolbar.

Add Print to the Quick Access Toolbar

It takes three clicks to print an email; you have to click File, then click Print, and then click Print again. You can reduce this sequence by one step if you add Print to the Quick Access Toolbar. (You can also avoid the File tab, which may unnerve you since it's so different from the others!)

1 Click the down arrow on the Quick Access Toolbar.

2 Click Print.

3 Note the new Print icon. Click it to print any selected email or calendar entry.

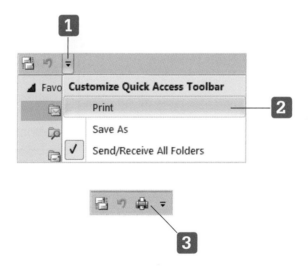

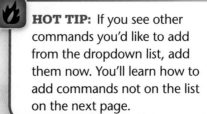

? DID YOU KNOW?

When a command is on the Quick Access Toolbar, it has a tick by it. Click any ticked item to remove it.

🔥 HOT TIP: If you see other commands you'd like to add from the dropdown list, add them now. You'll learn how to add commands not on the list on the next page.

Add New E-mail to the Quick Access Toolbar

When in a view such as Calendar, Contacts, or Tasks, creating a new email message requires you to click New Items, and then E-Mail Message. Otherwise, you have to return to Mail view and click New E-mail. You can create a new email much more quickly than that by adding the New E-Mail command to the Quick Access Toolbar. Once added, you can easily create a new email with a single click instead of several, and in any view or from any tab.

1 Click the arrow on the Quick Access Toolbar and click More Commands.

2 Under Choose commands from:, select All Commands.

3 Use the scroll bar to review the available commands.

4 When you see a command you want to add, click it.

5 Click Add.

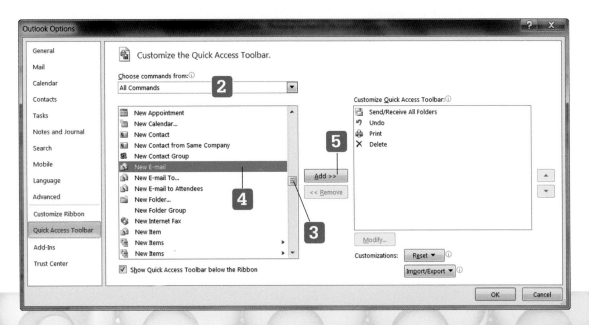

6 Repeat steps 3 to 5 as desired, adding commands you will use often.

7 Click OK. Note the new items we've added to the Quick Access Toolbar.

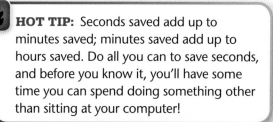 **HOT TIP:** Seconds saved add up to minutes saved; minutes saved add up to hours saved. Do all you can to save seconds, and before you know it, you'll have some time you can spend doing something other than sitting at your computer!

HOT TIP: Consider adding the following commands: Add Reminder, Block Sender, Calendar, Contacts, Daily Task List, Delete All, Junk, New Note, New Task, Not Junk, any relevant Search items, and To-Do Bar.

Add a custom group

If the icons on the Quick Access Toolbar are too small to see, you can add the commands you use often to a custom group you create on the Ribbon. When you configure Outlook with the commands you use most often, you work more efficiently, and thus, more quickly.

1 Right-click the Quick Access Toolbar and click Customize the Ribbon.

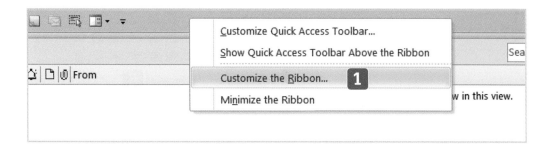

2 In Choose Commands from: select All Commands.

3 In the right pane, under Main Tabs, click Home (Mail). The new group will appear on the Home tab in Mail view. (Select another tab if desired.)

4 Click New Group, and then click Rename.

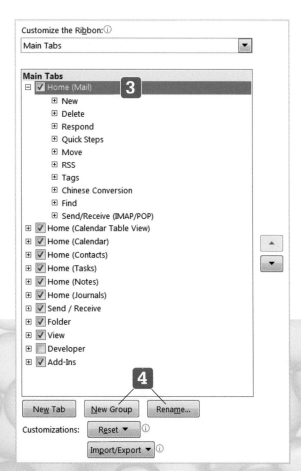

5 Type a display name for the group and choose an icon for it.

6 Click OK.

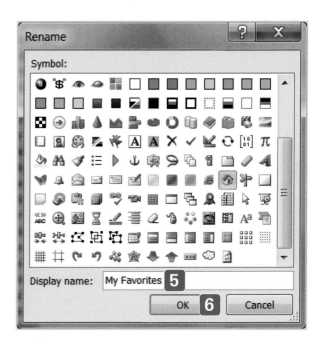

7 Select the new group and use the Up arrow to position it on the tab where desired.

8 Click OK. Note the new group on the appropriate tab on the Ribbon.

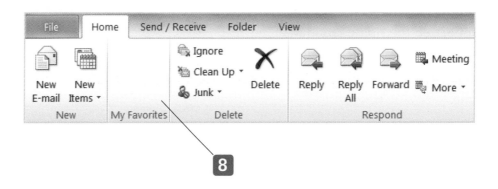

HOT TIP: You won't have any commands in the new group until you add them manually.

DID YOU KNOW?

Right-click the new group and choose Add to Quick Access Toolbar, and the icon you selected for the new group will appear there.

Add your favourite commands to the custom group

With a new custom group created, you can now add commands to it. Think of commands that you use often or those you'd like to use, such as Block Sender, Help, Junk, Add Reminder, New Note, New Task, or Daily Task List. If the commands are easily available you're more likely to incorporate them.

1 Right-click your new group and click Customize the Ribbon.

2 From the Choose commands from: options, select All Commands.

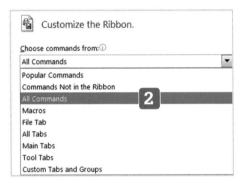

3 Scroll through the commands, until you find one you want to add. Click it.

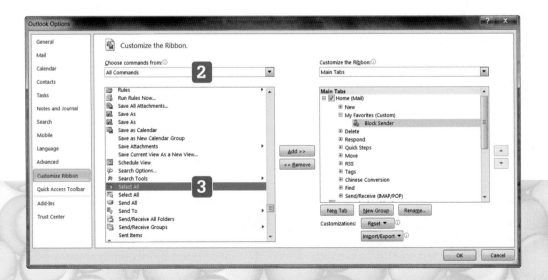

4 Click the new group in the right pane.

5 Click Add.

6 Repeat as desired.

7 Click OK. Note the new arrangement on the Ribbon.

HOT TIP: If you are forgetful, consider adding and using the New Note or New Task commands, and use them regularly.

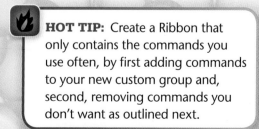

HOT TIP: Create a Ribbon that only contains the commands you use often, by first adding commands to your new custom group and, second, removing commands you don't want as outlined next.

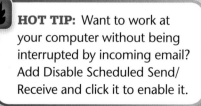

HOT TIP: Want to work at your computer without being interrupted by incoming email? Add Disable Scheduled Send/Receive and click it to enable it.

Remove an item from the Ribbon

There are quite a few commands on the Ribbon that you'll likely never use. For instance, if you know you'll never use anything on the View tab, you can completely remove it. If you use the View tab but never use the Arrangement tab *group*, you can remove only that.

1 Right-click the Quick Access Toolbar and click Customize the Ribbon.

2 To remove an entire tab, remove the tick by the tab.

3 To remove a single tab group from a tab:

   a Expand the tab by clicking the plus sign.

   b Click the tab group to remove.

   c Click Remove.

4 To reposition commands or tabs:

- Select the command or tab to move.

- Click the up and down arrows to move the command.

5 Click OK.

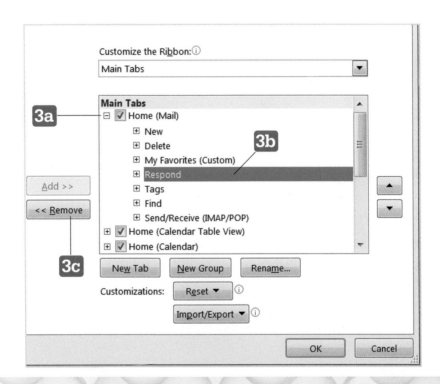

? DID YOU KNOW?

You can click New Tab and create an entirely new tab, populating it with custom groups.

🔥 HOT TIP: To reset all tabs and commands to their defaults, in the Customize the Ribbon window, click Reset All Customizations.

Understand the Outlook .pst file

Outlook stores its data in what's referred to as a .pst file. This file is tucked away deep inside your computer's hard drive, as shown here. The data is very important, and includes your contacts, folders, and mail, among other things. If you had a computer crash and lost this information, you could find yourself in quite a fix and, possibly, unable to retrieve what went missing.

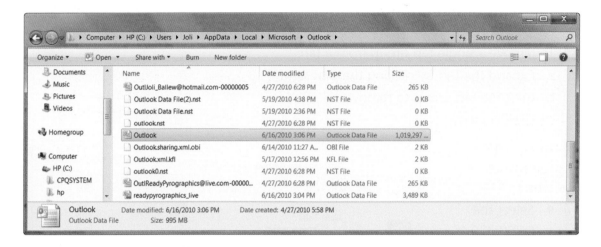

The .pst file includes the following data:

- emails inside local Outlook folders including Inbox, Sent Items, Outbox, and Deleted Items, among others
- contacts and contact information you've input
- calendar events, appointments, and other calendar data
- folders and subfolders you've created and the data in them.

? DID YOU KNOW?
.pst stands for Personal STore.

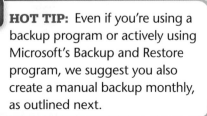

HOT TIP: Even if you're using a backup program or actively using Microsoft's Backup and Restore program, we suggest you also create a manual backup monthly, as outlined next.

Back up Outlook data

Data you store in Outlook can be quite valuable. You have email messages and contacts, of course, but you may also have pictures that came as attachments in emails, folders and subfolders you've created, receipts you're saving for tax time, lab results from doctors, and software codes for applications you've purchased online. If you lost it all, you'd have trouble getting it all back; it's best to create a regular backup schedule.

1 Click the File tab, and click Open.

2 Click Import.

ALERT: Save the backup to an external drive you can move away from your computer or off-site to keep the data on it safe.

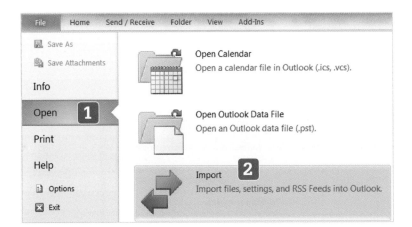

3 Click Export to a file; click Next.

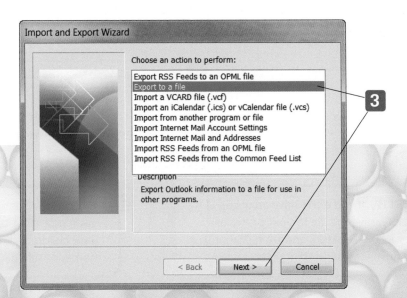

4 Click Outlook Data File (.pst) and click Next. (This is not shown.)

5 Click Personal Folders, verify Include Subfolders is ticked, and click Next.

6 Click Browse.

7 Browse to the location to save the file to, preferably an external drive or network drive.

8 Name the file and click OK.

9 Leave Replace duplicates with items imported selected and click Finish.

10 If desired, create a password when prompted and click OK.

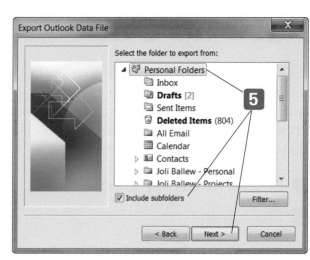

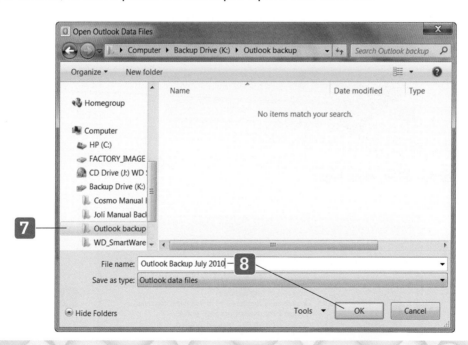

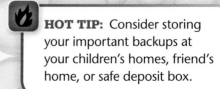 **HOT TIP:** If you don't have a backup drive available, save the file to your personal folder or the Desktop, and then drag it to a flash drive for safe-keeping later.

HOT TIP: Consider storing your important backups at your children's homes, friend's home, or safe deposit box.

Export your address book

If you get a second computer and set up email on it, you'll probably want to copy your address book to it. You may not want to copy your entire .pst file (or you may not be able to due to compatibility issues). To copy just your email addresses and nothing else, in Outlook, you need to "export" your address book to a flash drive (or network drive), and then, at the new computer, "import" the data you've copied.

1 Click the File tab, and click Open.

2 Click Import.

3 Select Export to a file; click Next.

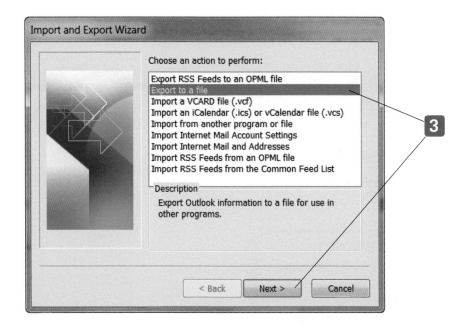

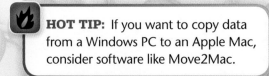

HOT TIP: If you want to copy data from a Windows PC to an Apple Mac, consider software like Move2Mac.

4 In the next screen, select Comma Separated Values (Windows), and click Next.

5 Click Contacts, and click Next.

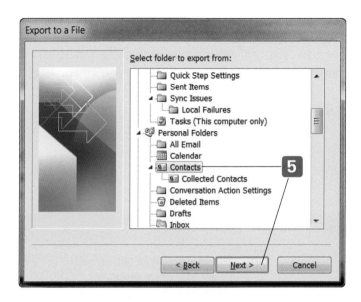

6 Click Browse, and navigate to the location to save the file to.

7 Name the file and click OK.

8 Click Next and Finish.

? DID YOU KNOW?

If you sync a mobile device like an iPad or BlackBerry, you can use the software that came with the device to sync contacts between it and Outlook.

! ALERT: To import the data, at the second computer, open the email program. Click the File tab and look for an Import command (what you see will vary depending on the program you're using on the second computer). Select Internet Mail and Addresses (or something similar), Comma Separated Values (Windows), locate the file, and complete the importing process.

Archive messages

Archiving allows you to move older messages to another location on your hard drive, which helps you manage how large your mailbox is. Maintaining Outlook in this manner allows it to run more smoothly and faster.

1 Click the File tab, and verify Info is selected.

2 Click Cleanup Tools.

3 Click Archive.

4 Verify Archive this folder and all subfolders is selected and click Personal Folders.

5 Click OK.

? DID YOU KNOW?
You'll notice a new folder called Archives in Outlook's Folder list. Expand the folder to access archived items.

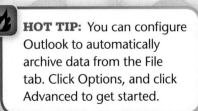

HOT TIP: You can configure Outlook to automatically archive data from the File tab. Click Options, and click Advanced to get started.

Learn more

There's a lot more to Outlook than we could ever introduce in three chapters. If you'd like to know more, there are several places to look.

- Click the Help icon (question mark in blue circle) in Outlook to access the Help files.

- Visit http://office.microsoft.com.
- Take an intermediate or advanced course at a local community college or senior citizens centre.
- Explore advanced books that only cover Outlook.

 DID YOU KNOW?

Microsoft employees regularly blog about new features, updates, and security patches for Office at Microsoft.com. Features and updates are generally enhancements to the program, while security patches help seal security breaches that arise over time.

HOT TIP: If you'll use the Calendar to manage your events, and create tasks and notes regularly, you'll be well on your way to getting the most you can from Outlook.

8 Introduction to Microsoft Excel

Open a new workbook from a template   147

Input data into cells   149

Use Zoom   150

Make cell data easier to see   151

Edit the contents in a cell   153

View another worksheet   154

Save a workbook   155

Open a new, blank workbook   156

Create headings for a monthly expenses budget   157

Create budget categories   158

Input budget approximations   159

Get the sum of a column of numbers   160

Get the average of a column of numbers   162

Copy and paste a formula   164

Get Help   165

Opt for templates   167

Introduction

Microsoft Excel is a spreadsheet program for storing, organising, manipulating, and calculating data you enter. That's the technical explanation. You use Excel to enter actual numbers and data and to manage that data. You can use Excel to input your income and approximate monthly expenses, and then review the information to see how you can better manage your money. You can create an inventory of household items and their values to create a document for your insurance company, solicitor, or heirs. You can create profit and loss statements for an accountant, a donation receipt for a charity, an expenses report for expenses accrued while performing consultancy work, and more.

You work in Excel in a workbook, and each workbook contains worksheets. You input data into the worksheet cells. You can format cells as you can format text, by applying font types, sizes, and colours, but you also have the option to format how numbers look in a cell. Once data has been entered, you can perform calculations with it, such as adding all items in a column, averaging items in a row, or performing more complex tasks like calculating accrued interest, interest rates, and loan and payment information.

Open a new workbook from a template

When you started using Microsoft Word, you probably started with a blank document. You could do that with Excel, too, but basic tasks in Excel will be easier to grasp if you start with a template instead. A template contains some information already, such as headings, placeholder data, and preconfigured calculations, and will help you understand how to use Excel more quickly.

1 Open Excel.

2 Click the File tab and click New.

3 Type Blood Pressure in the Search Office.com for templates window. Press Enter on the keyboard.

! ALERT: It's best to work through this chapter in the order presented.

! ALERT: Microsoft changes the available templates regularly, so the ones used here may not be available to you.

 HOT TIP: Once you've learned a little about entering and formatting data in cells, you'll be more able to work in a blank workbook.

4 If it's available, double-click this Blood pressure tracker template; if not, select another.

5 Type your name in the space provided (if applicable).

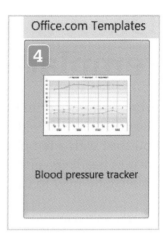

Office.com Templates

4

Blood pressure tracker

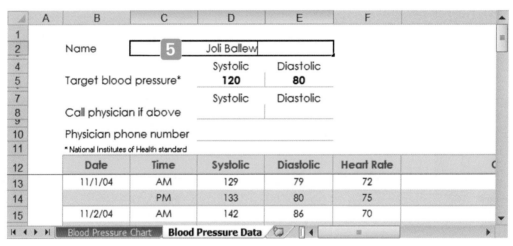

	A	B	C	D	E	F
1						
2		Name	5	Joli Ballew		
4				Systolic	Diastolic	
5		Target blood pressure*		120	80	
7				Systolic	Diastolic	
8		Call physician if above				
10		Physician phone number				
11		* National Institutes of Health standard				
12		Date	Time	Systolic	Diastolic	Heart Rate
13		11/1/04	AM	129	79	72
14			PM	133	80	75
15		11/2/04	AM	142	86	70

Blood Pressure Chart   **Blood Pressure Data**

HOT TIP: If you did not create a shortcut for Excel as outlined in Chapter 1, click Start, All Programs, Microsoft Office, and Microsoft Excel 2010.

Input data into cells

In a template, some cells are already populated with data. You can replace this data with your own. You can also input data into blank cells. Cells are defined by their location, where the row and column for the cell meet. Cell A1 is the top left cell in a worksheet.

1 Click in any unpopulated cell.

2 Type a number or a word.

149

? DID YOU KNOW?

Here we changed the Target blood pressure values in cells D5 and E5; you can make similar changes to any template, as desired.

	A	B	C	D	E	F
1						
2		Name		Joli Ballew		
4				Systolic	Diastolic	
5		Target blood pressure*		**115**	**75** 3	
7				Systolic	Diastolic	
8		Call physician if above		**160**	**100**	
9						
10		Physician phone number				

3 Click in any populated cell.

4 Type a number or a word.

🔥 HOT TIP: Consider changing the benchmarks for when to call a doctor, like we did in cells D8 and E8.

? DID YOU KNOW?

To delete contents in a cell, click inside the cell and click Delete on the keyboard.

Use Zoom

If you're having a hard time seeing what's in a cell (or on a chart or graph), the Zoom slider at the bottom of the page enables you to zoom in on the data. This doesn't change anything about the worksheet; the font size is not changed and cell size isn't altered; this only allows you to zoom in on data when you need to.

1 In any template or worksheet, locate the Zoom slider at the bottom of the page.

2 Move the slider to zoom in and out of data on the page.

3 You can also access Zoom from the View tab.

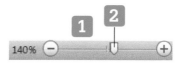

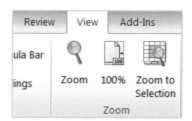

? DID YOU KNOW?

You can zoom in on a selected cell or item. From the View tab, click Zoom to Selection. Click 100% to return to the normal size.

Make cell data easier to see

You may have a hard time making out the contents of cells because the size of the cells is so small. You shouldn't have to put on your reading glasses to work in Excel and you shouldn't have to constantly access the Zoom commands. Although there are several ways to remedy this situation, you can opt to change the font size and reposition the rows and columns to accommodate the data.

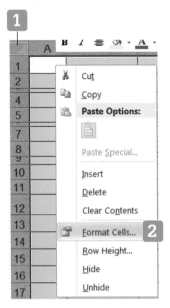

1 Click the triangle in the top right corner, next to row 1 and cell A, to select the entire worksheet.

2 Right-click inside the worksheet and click Format Cells.

3 From the Alignment tab, click Wrap text.

4 Click OK.

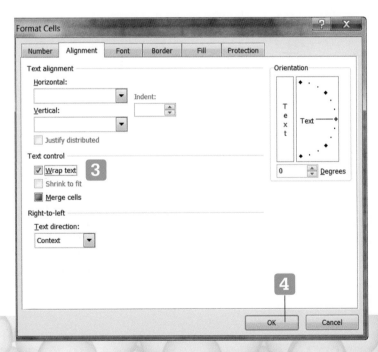

HOT TIP: If the font is hard for you to read, select a different font and change the font size.

? DID YOU KNOW?
You can also click Bold from the mini-toolbar.

5 Right-click again and select a larger font size from the mini-toolbar.

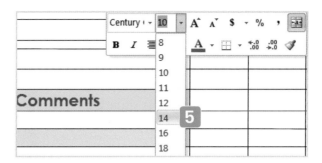

6 Click in any cell to deselect all.

7 Position the cursor in between any row or column divider until the two-headed arrow appears.

8 Drag to expand the cells so all of the text in the cells for that row or column shows.

Edit the contents in a cell

You can replace all of the data in a cell by clicking it once and typing the desired data. What you type replaces what's there. However, there are times when you only need to change a letter or a single number in a cell, or you simply want to add information to what's already there. In these cases you'd rather not replace everything, only the data that needs to be changed.

1 Double-click in a cell that contains data.

2 Click to place the cursor in the desired position in the cell.

> **1** **2** |Comments

3 Type to add data.

> **3** **Circumstances and** |**Comments**

DID YOU KNOW?

In this editing mode you can also select data by dragging your mouse over the data you want to change.

HOT TIP: When using a template, feel free to edit headings, fonts, font sizes, row and column size, and placeholder data as desired.

View another worksheet

Templates often have multiple worksheets. These will appear as tabs at the bottom of the Excel interface.

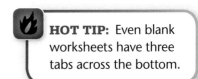

HOT TIP: Even blank worksheets have three tabs across the bottom.

1 In any template, look for additional tabs at the bottom of the Excel interface.

2 Click the tab to view its associated worksheet.

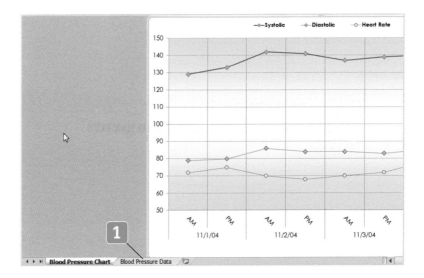

3 You can add a new sheet by clicking the empty tab next to the tabs shown.

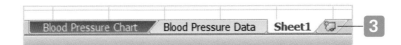

 **DID YOU KNOW?**
You can rename any worksheet by double-clicking its tab.

 HOT TIP: If the data in a worksheet runs horizontally off the page and out of view, use the horizontal scroll bar to the right of the tabs to view the data.

Save a workbook

You'll be prompted to save your work when you close Excel, but it's best to save it yourself from the File tab. Make sure to name the file with a descriptive name, like My Blood Pressure 2010 or something similar.

1 Click File and click Save As, this is above Info which is the default.

2 Type a name for the workbook.

3 Locate a folder to save the workbook to. If you're unsure, click Documents.

4 Click Save.

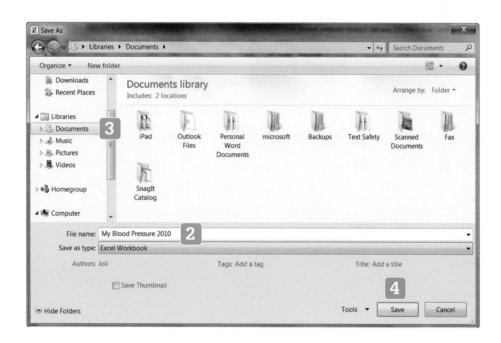

? DID YOU KNOW?

You can open the document later from the File tab, by clicking Open, and by browsing to the folder where you saved the file. Alternatively, you can click the File tab and click Recent.

HOT TIP: If you want to save and send the data, click the File tab, click Save & Send, and select the type of file desired. Click Send as PDF if you want to make it more difficult for the recipient to edit the file.

Open a new, blank workbook

Now that you know a little about inputting and editing cell data, you can experiment with creating a workbook from scratch. On this page and the ones following, you'll learn how to create a monthly expenses budget worksheet from a blank workbook.

1 In Excel, click the File tab.

2 Click New and click Blank Workbook.

3 Verify you can see the gridlines. If you can't, click View and tick Gridlines.

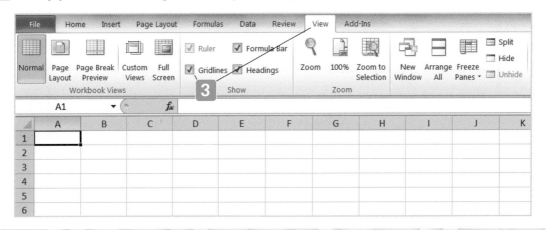

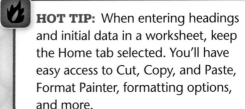

! ALERT: Work from here to the end of the chapter in the order it's presented. Each step builds on the step prior to it.

🔥 HOT TIP: When entering headings and initial data in a worksheet, keep the Home tab selected. You'll have easy access to Cut, Copy, and Paste, Format Painter, formatting options, and more.

Create headings for a monthly expenses budget

Think about your monthly expenses. Perhaps you have bills for utilities, satellite TV, internet, mobile phones, rent or mortgage, and car or other payments. You may also pay for credit cards, insurance, or even waste removal services. You may also pay a specific amount each month for prescriptions, or put away money for quarterly or yearly taxes.

1 In cell A1 type Monthly Expenses; position the column so that you can see both words.

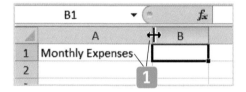

2 In cell B1 type the words Due Date; in cell C1 type Approximate Amount; in cell D1 type Payment Type. Position the columns as desired.

3 In cell E1, type January.

4 Position the cursor in the bottom right corner of E1 and when you see the + sign, drag right to P1. You'll see the months being added as you drag.

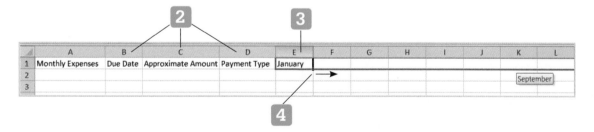

5 Click the File tab and click Save As. Save the workbook.

HOT TIP: To apply a font to all text in row A, click the 1 to left of Monthly Expenses. From the Home tab, select a font, font colour, and perhaps even a font size. Note that you may have to reposition the rows and columns after doing this.

HOT TIP: Sometimes it is helpful to leave a blank row to make the worksheet data easier to read.

Create budget categories

Now you can input your budget categories. As with column headings, feel free to format the text with fonts, colours, and perhaps even a background colour (from the Format dialog box under the Fill tab).

1 Input budget headings in cells A3, A4, A5, etc.

2 Select the cells by dragging your mouse over them.

3 Right-click the selected cells and click Format Cells.

4 Use the tabs to format the cells. Consider adding:
- From the Alignment tab, Wrap text.
- From the Font tab, Font Style Bold and Size 14.

5 Click OK.

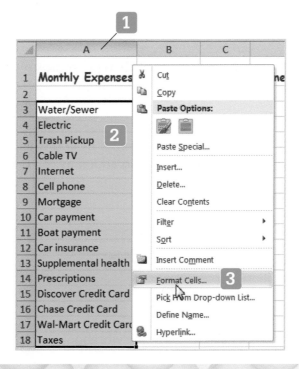

DID YOU KNOW?
You can perform a spell check on the worksheet from the Review tab. Click Spelling.

Input budget approximations

With headings in place you're ready to input your data. Simply click inside any cell and type the desired number. Later you'll learn to format the dates and numbers.

1 Click cell B3 and type a January date on which your first budget item must be paid.

2 Click cell C3 and type the approximate amount of the bill.

3 Click cell D3 and input how you pay the bill (credit card, cheque, direct debit, online).

4 Repeat these steps to input the other data.

HOT TIP: As you pay these bills each month, enter the exact amount in the appropriate cell.

? DID YOU KNOW?

If you need to insert a row or column, right-click a cell below or to the right of the row or column to add and click Insert. Then click Entire row or Entire column. Click OK. The row or column will be inserted above the row or before the column.

	A	B	C	D	E	F	G
1	Monthly Expenses	Date Due	Approximate Amount	Payment Type	January	February	March
2							
3	Water/Sewer	15/01/2010	80	Online de...	75	80	82
4	Electric	01/01/2010	200	Online debit	150	160	100
5	Trash Pickup	01/01/2010	15	Check	15	15	15
6	Cable TV	20/01/2010	140	Credit Card	140	140	141
7	Internet	05/01/2010	60	Auto deduct	60	60	60
8	Cell phone						
9	Mortgage						
10	Car payment						

HOT TIP: When inputting data, use the Tab key on the keyboard to move from cell to cell.

HOT TIP: Right-click any group of selected cells, columns, or rows, and click Format Cells. There you can choose the type of formatting you want to use for dates and currency, among others.

Get the sum of a column of numbers

The best thing about Excel is that you can configure it to perform calculations for you. One of the most common applications is to total a column of numbers – you'll want to calculate your spending totals for each month in your expenses budget worksheet.

1 Click inside the cell where you'd like the sum for a column of numbers to appear. This is likely a cell at the bottom of a column of numbers.

2 Click fx. (Additional icons will appear to the left of fx, and you will now see an X and a tick mark.)

3 Click Sum and click OK.

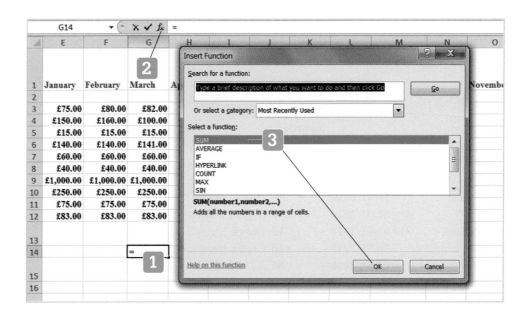

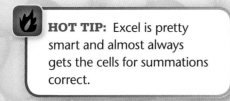

HOT TIP: Excel is pretty smart and almost always gets the cells for summations correct.

4 Review the cell numbers in the next dialog box. The first entry should represent the first cell in a list of numbers and the last entry should represent the last. If it does, click OK.

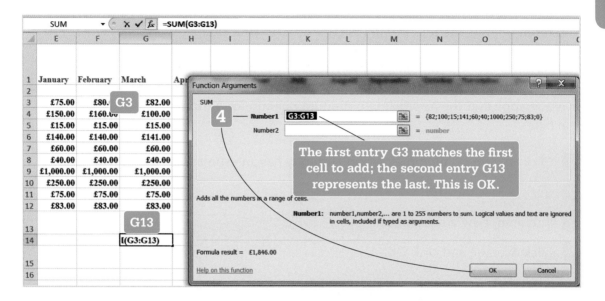

5 If the entry is not correct, drag your mouse over the cells to add. Click OK.

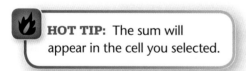

HOT TIP: The sum will appear in the cell you selected.

Get the average of a column of numbers

You input an estimate for each bill in column C of your budget worksheet when you set it up. You may have based that on what you recall paying last year, or what you paid last month. You can tell Excel to calculate the average of what you've paid each month so far (and input the result into your budget worksheet). You can then have this average appear in the Approximate Amount column for a more realistic estimation of the bill.

1 Click an item in column C, which currently has an estimate for the bill in the row.

2 Click fx (not shown).

3 If desired, type a description.

4 Click Average and click OK.

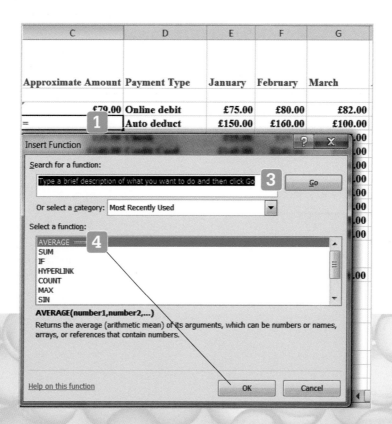

5 Use your mouse to drag over the cells you want to use to create an average and click OK.

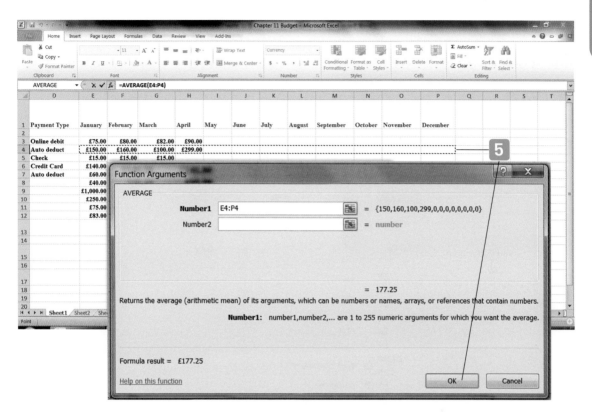

? DID YOU KNOW?
Each time you input new data, the average will be updated automatically, provided you selected all of the months when creating the formula.

! ALERT: If you input zeros in the empty cells, Excel will assume you want to include that zero in the calculation. Leave empty cells empty until you're ready to input valid data.

Copy and paste a formula

If you like how the sums and averages look in your worksheet you'll want to create them for each column of numbers and for each Approximate Amount entry. You can copy a formula from one cell and paste it to another to apply it in lieu of recreating it.

1. Click the cell that contains the sum for a set of numbers. This is the cell you configured the Sum formula for.

2. Right-click the cell and click Copy.

3. Right-click in a cell to apply the formula to, a cell at the bottom of a list of numbers you'd like to sum.

4. Note the Paste options. Click the Formula option, fx to paste the formula only.

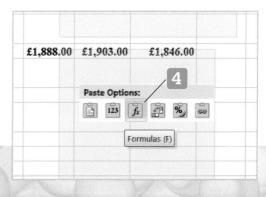

HOT TIP: If you created a formula in cell G14, to sum numbers from cells G3 to G13, see if you can apply the formula to similar sets of numbers in cell F14 or E14.

HOT TIP: If at first you don't succeed, try again in a different cell or with a different set of numbers. Working with formulas is a little tricky and takes time to master.

Get Help

When formatting goes awry, you may see all pound signs. When formulas go awry, you may get data that doesn't "add up". When there are other problems, you may see a triangle in a cell or what looks like a portion of a formula instead of data. In these instances, there is most likely an issue with the calculation or something amiss in your logic. Help is available, though.

1 If you see a triangle in a cell, click the cell. Then:

- Click the exclamation mark beside it.
- Review the information. (In this instance, we've omitted adjacent cells, which is OK.)

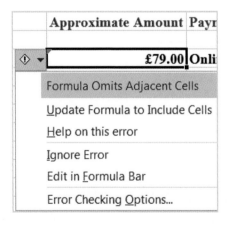

- Note the options to repair the problem. (In this case we can ignore the error.)

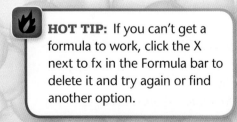

HOT TIP: If you can't get a formula to work, click the X next to fx in the Formula bar to delete it and try again or find another option.

2 If you see a formula in a cell:

- Click the exclamation mark if one exists. You'll then be able to review the problem and apply possible solutions.

- Click the cell to view what's missing from the formula. Often you need to specify the cells to use.

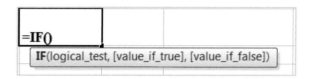

- Click the cell and click the command that appears below it. Here, you'd click If. You can then review the Help files.

 HOT TIP: When you create a formula and it's incomplete, you'll be prompted regarding the error. You have the option to click Help at that time.

HOT TIP: If you create a formula to average a set of numbers and include cells that aren't numbers, but instead dates or text, you may still get a number, albeit an incorrect one.

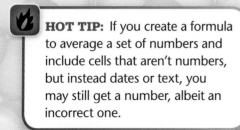

Opt for templates

Now that you've tried to create your own budget expenses sheet you may be more convinced than ever that working from a template is the best solution for populating common Excel spreadsheets. Before ending this chapter, then, take a look at the templates categorised under Budgets.

1 Click the File tab.

2 Click New.

3 Double-click Budgets.

4 Click each budget in the Office.com templates to preview it.

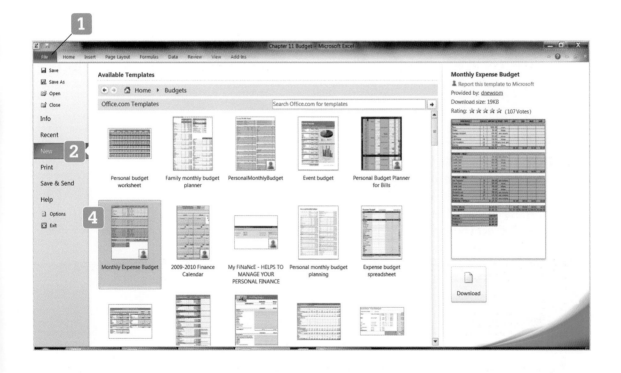

 ALERT: You must be online to access the Office.com templates.

 ALERT: Templates change often, so what you see here may no longer be available.

5 Double-click the template to download it.

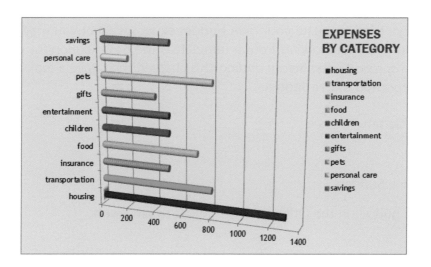

 HOT TIP: There are lots of budgets that also include charts and tables already built-in. These change as you add data to reflect your personal budget and spending habits.

9 Manage and edit workbooks

Name or rename a worksheet   171

Insert rows and columns   172

Delete and hide rows and columns   173

Merge cells   174

Select a range of data   175

Apply a conditional format to a range   176

Convert a range to a bar chart   177

Convert a range to a line chart   178

Add titles and data labels to a chart   179

Write your own formula   180

Get help with formulas   181

Introduction

Excel is a very powerful program and enables you to create complex spreadsheets and perform intricate calculations with the data you collect. You can use Excel as a publishing program too, to create invoices, flyers, and calendars, and as a word-processing program to create and print labels, stationery, and memos. All of this is most easily achieved with a template.

Templates are starting points, though; you'll often find you need to add quite a few of your own touches (or start your own workbook from scratch). Whichever you choose, at some point you'll need to add your own rows or columns, format the data you input, apply "conditional" formatting to highlight data that meets certain criteria you set, and perform other editing tasks to make the worksheet unique and useful. You can enhance your work with charts to represent your data and even create your own formulas. You'll learn how to do all of that here and more.

Name or rename a worksheet

There are tabs at the bottom of each Excel workbook you create. By default, they are named Sheet 1, Sheet 2, and Sheet 3. That's not very descriptive. You can rename the tabs to better represent what each tab contains.

1 In Excel, click the File tab, click New, and click Blank workbook.

2 Right-click Sheet 1, Sheet 2, or Sheet 3.

3 Click Rename.

4 Name the tab as desired.

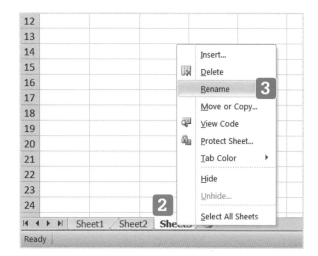

> **HOT TIP:** Name the tab so you can easily decipher the data on the worksheet.

> **? DID YOU KNOW?**
> When you create a new, blank workbook it contains three tabs, each of which represents a worksheet. You can add or delete tabs by right-clicking on their name.

> **HOT TIP:** Right-click any tab and click Tab Colour to add a colour to the tab name.

Insert rows and columns

There will be times when you need to insert rows and columns. Generally this happens when you realise you need to input additional data after the fact, such as adding a Country column to a worksheet that contains contact information, or adding a body fat column to a diet and exercise worksheet. (Hopefully you aren't adding a Late Fee column to a budget worksheet!)

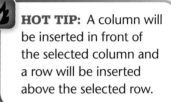

HOT TIP: A column will be inserted in front of the selected column and a row will be inserted above the selected row.

1 Click the row or column title you'd like to insert a row or column in front of.

2 Right-click and select Insert.

	F	G	H	I
	Notes	Blood Sugar		Minutes
	Doctor Appt.	124 after candy		Minimal
		98 before bed		75
				50
		108 AM Fasting		40
				60
				4 hours

Cut
Copy
Paste Options:
Paste Special...
Insert
Delete
Clear Contents
Format Cells

3 Name or format the new column as desired.

E	F	G	H
BP/Calorie Burn	Notes	Body Fat	Blood Sugar
117/72	Doctor Appt.		124 after candy

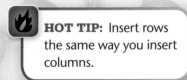

HOT TIP: Insert rows the same way you insert columns.

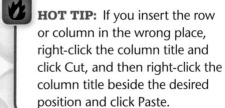

HOT TIP: If you insert the row or column in the wrong place, right-click the column title and click Cut, and then right-click the column title beside the desired position and click Paste.

Delete and hide rows and columns

When working with a template, you'll often find that you don't need all the rows and columns. Perhaps you want to delete columns for student loans, child care, or rent (when filling out a budget worksheet) or delete certain days from a time sheet because your business is not open then. Perhaps you want to hide data from those who may view the worksheet or refrain from printing certain cells while still keeping the data available when you need it.

1 Click the row or column title to delete or hide, such as A, B, or C, or 1, 2, or 3.

2 Right-click and select Hide or Delete.

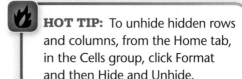

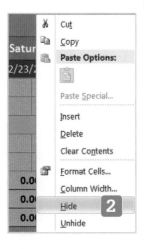

HOT TIP: To unhide hidden rows and columns, from the Home tab, in the Cells group, click Format and then Hide and Unhide.

HOT TIP: To select multiple rows or columns, hold down the Shift key while selecting those that are contiguous or the Ctrl key when selecting those that are non-contiguous.

WHAT DOES THIS MEAN?

Delete: To completely remove a row or column. To replace the column you'd have to recreate it.

Hide: To hide a row or column so it doesn't show, with the option to "unhide" when needed. Data that is input in the column is not erased, only hidden.

Merge cells

Sometimes a heading really needs to cover two or more columns for the purpose of organising the data below it (or beside it). You can see here that the days of the week each encompass two cells. This allows the creator to better lay out the rest of the worksheet.

E	F	G	H	I	J
Sunday		Monday		Tuesday	
2/17/2008		2/18/2008		2/19/2008	
15:00:00	Total		Total		Total
21:00:00	6.00		0.00		0.00

1 Type the desired information into the left-most cell you want to use.

2 Leave the adjacent cells to the right (the ones you plan to merge) empty.

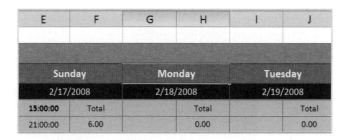

3 Select both cells.

4 From the Home tab, click Merge and Center.

5 Format the text as desired.

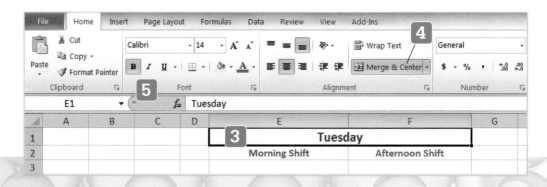

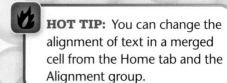 **HOT TIP:** You can split merged cells. Just select the larger cell and, from the Home tab, click the arrow by Merge and Center and click Unmerge Cells.

HOT TIP: You can change the alignment of text in a merged cell from the Home tab and the Alignment group.

Select a range of data

When you're ready to sort, organise, or perform calculations with data, you must select the range of data you want to work with first. Once selected, you can sort the data alphabetically, highlight data that meets a certain benchmark you set, view the data in a chart or graph, and more. There are various ways to select data.

- Drag your mouse over the consecutive data to select. You may select a range of numbers or a group of data that includes descriptions and numbers.

1	**2010 BUDGET**	**DATES**	**AMOUNTS**
2	**HOUSEHOLD BILLS**		
3	Rent	1	1000.00
4	Water	1	20.00
5	Savings Account	1	400.00
6	Cable	5	124.00
7	Cell Phone	11	150.00
8	Car Insurance	22	110.00
9	Electric	27	150.00

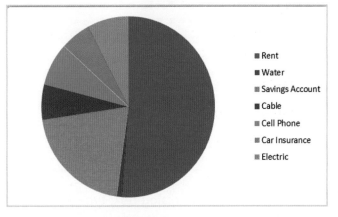

- Rent
- Water
- Savings Account
- Cable
- Cell Phone
- Car Insurance
- Electric

 HOT TIP: When you select a group of data such as bill type and amount, you can then use the selected data to populate a chart of graph.

- Select numbers in various columns by holding down the Ctrl key while dragging your mouse to select. You may select multiple cells to apply the same formatting to them all.
- Select data in a list by clicking the first item in a list, holding down the Shift key, and selecting the last. You may select multiple data to sort or alphabetise it.

 HOT TIP: When inputting data, strive to make data in columns and rows have similar, relevant content. For instance, when inputting weight in a fitness spreadsheet, only put the number and don't include additional information in the same cell (such as Before Bed or At Doctor). This additional data makes it impossible to perform calculations with the data later.

Apply a conditional format to a range

You can quickly scan a worksheet to find data that is above or below a specific number you set, data that contains specific text, data that is before or after a specific date, data that is in between two numbers, and data that is in the top or bottom percentage in a set of data.

1 Select the range of data to review.

2 From the Home tab, click Conditional Formatting.

HOT TIP: Repeat these steps to apply conditional formatting for other items in the Highlight Cell Rules options and in the Top/Bottom Rules options.

3 Click Highlight Cell Rules, and click Greater Than.

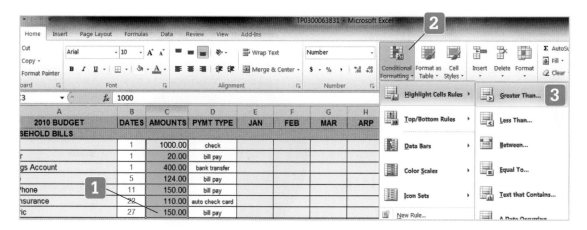

4 In the Greater Than dialog box, type a threshold number.

5 Select a formatting colour.

6 Note the changes in the document and click OK to apply.

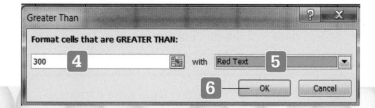

 HOT TIP: Use conditional formatting to locate data such as any worker who is nearing overtime hours and pay for the week, a price that is outside of your budget, a principal or interest threshold in an amortisation worksheet, or items in your home inventory that are valued above a price you set.

Convert a range to a bar chart

A bar chart allows the reader to draw conclusions more quickly than by simply reading the data in a worksheet. To create a bar chart you need at least two criteria; for instance, biscuit types and number of boxes sold.

1 Select two ranges of data.

Caramel deLights	Peanut Butter Patties	Shortbread	Thin Mints	Peanut Butter Sandwich	Thanks-A-Lot	Lemonades	Cinna-Spins
			2			1	
							2
			2		3		
1	1	1	1	1	1	1	1

2 Click the Insert tab.

3 Click Bar, and select a bar chart type.

4 Select and delete the legend if it doesn't suit you, or change the colours in the chart from the Chart Tools tabs.

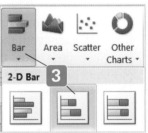

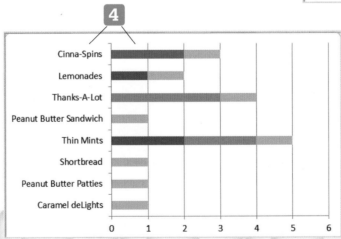

Convert a range to a line chart

Line charts can be helpful in situations where you need to show data as trends that happen over time. You might use a line chart to map blood pressure levels over a long period of time, for instance.

1 Select a group of data to graph.

2 Click the Insert tab.

3 Click Line Chart.

4 Select a line chart to apply.

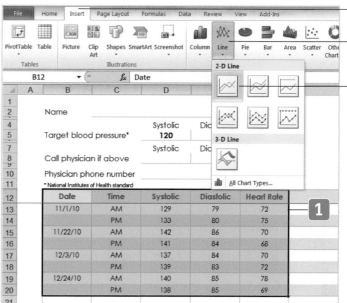

HOT TIP: Your charts probably won't be perfect right away. You'll have to experiment with the data you choose to get the chart just right.

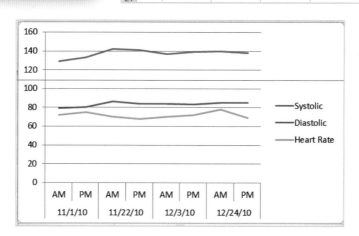

HOT TIP: Because the line chart represents longer periods of time, the data may appear too close together. Drag from the bottom corners, sides, or top of the chart to increase its size and spread out the data.

? DID YOU KNOW?

When you change data in your worksheet, data is changed automatically in the chart. You do not have to recreate it.

Add titles and data labels to a chart

Data labels are what define the data in a chart. You can edit the labels Excel inputs or create your own. One of the things you can input are axis titles for the horizontal and/ or vertical axes. You can also create a chart title, and add data labels to make the data easier to understand.

1 Select the chart.

2 From the Chart Tools tabs, select Layout.

3 Click Chart Title, click Above Chart.

4 Type a chart name and press Enter on the keyboard.

5 Click Axis Titles, click Primary Horizontal Axis Title, and click Title Below Axis.

6 Type a title and click Enter on the keyboard.

7 Click Data Labels, and click Above.

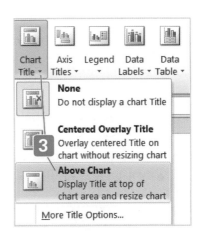

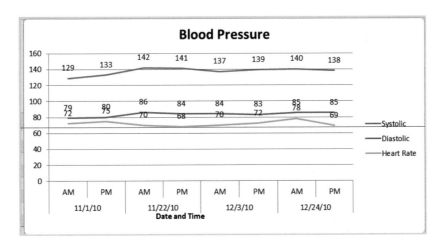

HOT TIP: It's still easier to start from a template that includes the charts already built in. You can see if there are charts available in a template by previewing it.

HOT TIP: Try out Trendline options. Excel will draw a line denoting trends for data streams. You can then tell if data is generally rising or falling, for instance.

Write your own formula

As you've learned, starting from a template is the easiest way to start a worksheet. Templates will have formulas already entered for complicated calculations. You already know how to get the sum and the average of numbers on your own, though, and you can expand on that to create other formulas with practice.

1 Click in a cell where you'd like to insert a formula you create.

2 From the Home tab, click inside the fx window.

3 Input the function:

- Type an = sign.
- Type any appropriate mathematical symbols, such as parentheses.
- To input a variable, use the cell name.
- Click Enter on the keyboard.

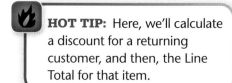

HOT TIP: Here, we'll calculate a discount for a returning customer, and then, the Line Total for that item.

ALERT: You must do the calculation manually to verify it is correct.

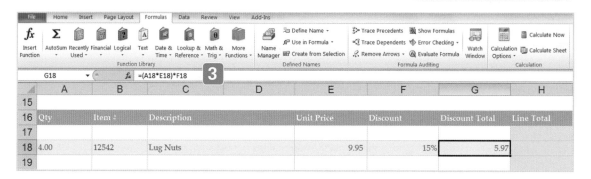

4 Repeat to add another function.

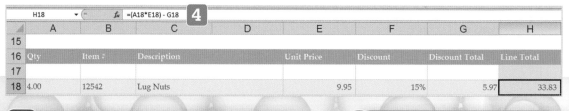

HOT TIP: Write down the formula on paper before trying to type it into the fx window. For Discount Total, we need to multiply the quantity by the unit price and multiply the total by the discount.

DID YOU KNOW?
You can copy and paste these formulas to related cells in the worksheet.

Get help with formulas

Writing your own formulas is difficult, especially if you're new to Excel. There is help, though. Here are a few options:

- From the Formulas tab, click Insert Function. Type a little about what you want to do and click Go. The first formula in the list is often a good place to start.

- Click F1 to open the Help window. In the Search window, type Functions.

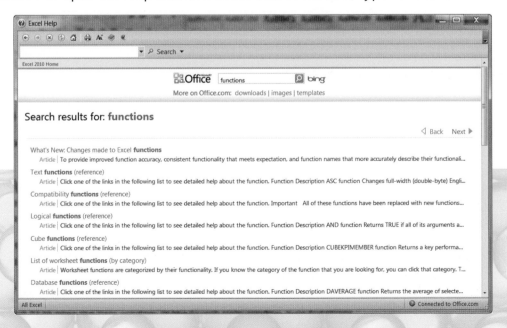

● Click the yellow exclamation mark that appears by a non-functioning or questionable function or formula.

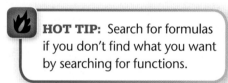

50.00%		40.00%
168,00(⬦▾		#VALUE!
	Error in Value	
VALUE	Help on this error	
	Show Calculation Steps...	
15%	Ignore Error	
	Edit in Formula Bar	
5	Error Checking Options...	
30%		

HOT TIP: Search for formulas if you don't find what you want by searching for functions.

10 Share, print, and personalise

Save a workbook   185

Change the file type   186

Create a PDF document   187

Protect a workbook   188

Send a workbook in an email   189

Use Print Preview   190

Explore Page Setup   192

Print a workbook   193

Change where files save by default   194

Personalise the Quick Access Toolbar   196

Customise the Ribbon   197

Learn more   199

Introduction

Now that you've had some experience with Excel, you're ready to save, share, and print the workbooks you've created. As with other Microsoft Office programs, you can save files in various formats and you can protect your work by applying a password, permissions, or encryption. You can send files via email, upload them to a web site, and print the documents you need to physically share or put in the post.

You can personalise Excel too. You probably already have a good idea which commands you use the most, and which commands you will likely never use. You can add your favourite commands to Excel's Quick Access Toolbar and personalise the Ribbon by rearranging tabs and tab groups, or creating your own.

Save a workbook

You save workbooks so that you can access them later. Workbooks are saved in the Excel Workbook file format by default, but you can select another option if desired. For instance, if you know you're going to share the file with a friend who uses Excel 97, you can save in the Excel 97-2003 Workbook format. If you know you're going to be posting the data to the web, you can save in Web Page format.

1 In Excel, click the File tab and click Save As.

2 Browse to the location of the folder to store the file.

3 Double-click the folder to open it.

4 Click Save.

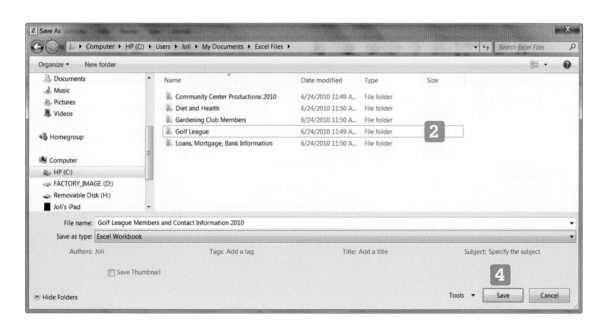

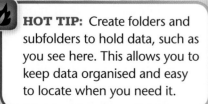

HOT TIP: Create folders and subfolders to hold data, such as you see here. This allows you to keep data organised and easy to locate when you need it.

DID YOU KNOW?

If you use Windows Vista or Windows 7, you can locate any file by clicking the Start orb in the bottom left corner of the screen and typing in the file name.

Change the file type

You can change the file type anytime you need to. You may need to make the file compatible with older office programs so others can access them, change the file to text or comma delimited so you can print the data on to labels, print envelopes, or import the data into another program, or save the file so that it can be opened by programs that aren't from Microsoft, like OpenDocument.

1 Click the File tab.

2 Click Save & Send.

3 Click Change File Type.

4 Select the file type.

5 Click Save As.

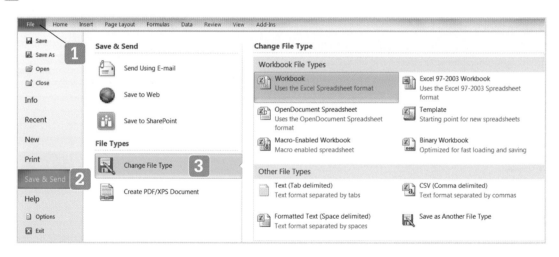

WHAT DOES THIS MEAN?

Comma delimited, Tab delimited: A text format that can be read by most computer programs. You might export your contacts in Outlook as comma delimited, and then import them in Excel using the same format.

OpenDocument: A format used in free and open source programs such as OpenOffice.org and NeoOffice. If you know you'll be sharing a file with someone who uses these programs, save it in this format first.

Create a PDF document

To present your document to virtually anyone in the world and to keep it from being easily modified, save your document as a PDF (Portable Document Format). Use PDF to send data to professional printers, professional organisations, or to anyone who uses a Mac, Linux, or other non-Windows-based computer. PDF files preserve formatting and fonts, so the document appears the same to the recipient as it does to you.

1 Click the File tab and click Save & Send.

2 Click Create PDF/XPS Document.

3 Click Create PDF/XPS.

4 Click Publish.

 DID YOU KNOW?
Recipients often open PDF files with a free program called Adobe Reader.

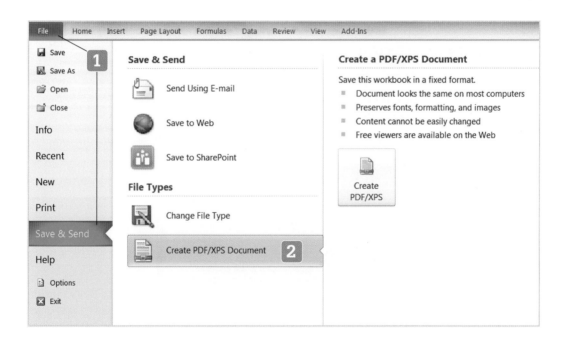

WHAT DOES THIS MEAN?

XPS: The XML Paper Specification format. Similar to PDF, it retains formatting, can be read on virtually any computer, and is a "final" document ready for printing or publishing. This is how you'll send flyers, playbills, brochures and the like to a professional print shop.

Protect a workbook

If you've created a legal, sensitive, or binding document in Excel, such as an invoice, expenses report, inventory list, or financial statement, and need to share it with others, you have to make sure that the recipient can't alter the data in your document. You have to protect yourself. You do that by applying security protection on the Excel worksheet you need to share.

1 Open the document to protect and click the File tab.

2 Click the Info tab if it isn't already selected.

3 Click Protect Workbook.

4 Select the desired protection.

5 Complete the process by inputting the required information, which will differ depending on what you selected in Step 4.

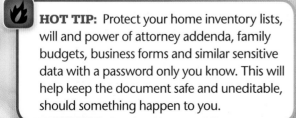

HOT TIP: Protect your home inventory lists, will and power of attorney addenda, family budgets, business forms and similar sensitive data with a password only you know. This will help keep the document safe and uneditable, should something happen to you.

ALERT: If you do protect your work with passwords, make sure to write down the password and keep it somewhere safe, but away from prying eyes, identity thieves, or unscrupulous family members or co-workers.

Send a workbook in an email

When you're ready to share a workbook you can email it. You may email a workbook that contains the cast and crew for a play you're producing, the members of your ladies' golf team and their contact information, or even an invoice you've created for a company you own, to name a few examples.

1 Open the workbook to email and click the File tab.

2 Click Save & Send.

3 Click Send Using E-Mail.

4 Note all of the ways you can send the worksheet and select one.

5 Complete the email and send it.

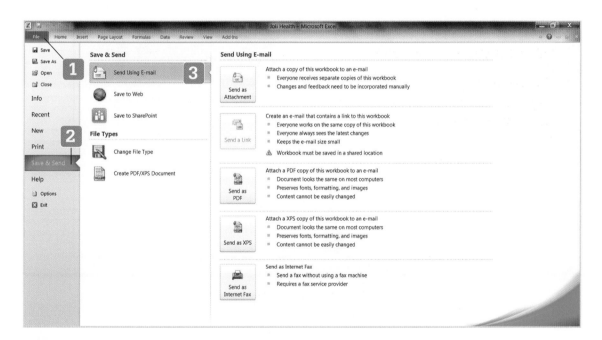

HOT TIP: Remember to protect worksheets before emailing them if you don't want the recipient to be able to edit them and change your data. Alternatively, you can send as a PDF or XPS file during the email attachment process. (Note, though, that if someone really wants to edit the data, they can find a way.)

DID YOU KNOW?

You can send worksheets as faxes, but you need to subscribe to a fax service and meet their connection requirements. You can opt to print and then fax the document the old-fashioned way if you don't have this set up.

Use Print Preview

If you need to manually fax a worksheet, put it in the post, or physically hand it to another person, you have to print the worksheet. Before you commit, though, use Print Preview to verify what you're about to print is exactly what you need.

1 Click the File tab and click Print.

2 If there are multiple pages, click to preview each page.

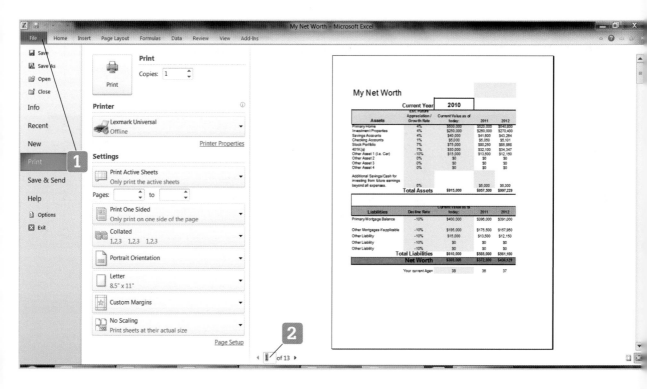

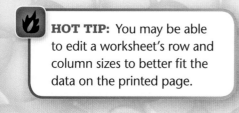

HOT TIP: You may be able to edit a worksheet's row and column sizes to better fit the data on the printed page.

3 If the printout isn't going to look the way you want it to, try the following.

- Switch from Portrait Orientation to Landscape Orientation.
- Select a new paper size, 8½ × 14 say, instead of 8½ × 11.
- Select Print Entire Workbook instead of Print Active Sheets.
- Select Narrow Margins.
- Try various scaling options.

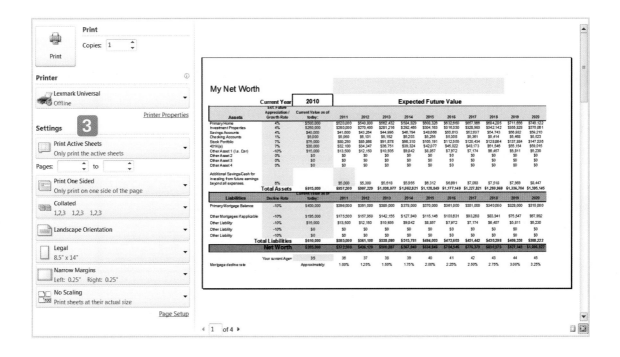

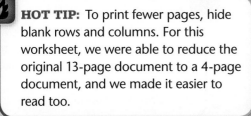

HOT TIP: To print fewer pages, hide blank rows and columns. For this worksheet, we were able to reduce the original 13-page document to a 4-page document, and we made it easier to read too.

Explore Page Setup

If you were unable to get the perfect fit for your data using the Print Preview techniques just introduced, you may be able to make improvements using Page Setup. Here you can add headers and footers, change the print resolution, and perform additional tasks (although much of what you'll see here is also available in Print Preview).

1. Click the File tab, and click Print.

2. Click Page Setup.

3. Note the tabs, and click each one.

4. Apply formatting changes as desired.

5. Click OK.

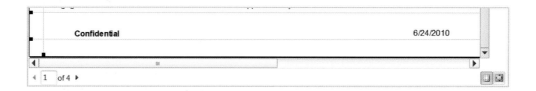

HOT TIP: When you apply changes using the Print Preview window (see previous page), you can see the changes as you apply them. With the Page Setup dialog box, you have to apply the changes first, which adds steps and takes more time.

HOT TIP: In Print Preview in the bottom right area of the window there are icons that enable you to see the margins and zoom in on your document, for instance, to preview new headers or footers.

Print a workbook

Once you're ready to print, click Print! Note that once printed, security measures such as the inability to open the document without a password are moot, and anyone could copy and input the data into their own spreadsheet to later alter it.

1 Click the File tab, and click Print.

2 Note the Print Preview.

3 Click Print.

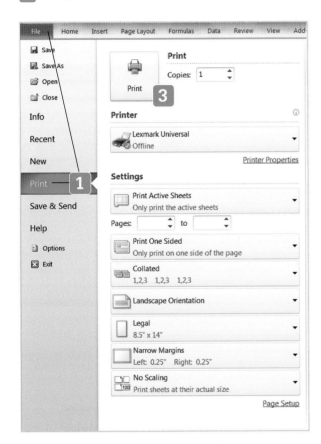

ALERT: The sync settings you have configured for devices like iPads and PDAs may, by default, copy sensitive documents to these devices, especially if you keep these documents in your Documents folder or Documents Library. Be safe and double-check that these documents aren't being copied to devices that can be easily lost or stolen.

HOT TIP: Print important documents and store them in a safe place, like a safe deposit box, lawyer's office, or fireproof/theft-proof safe.

ALERT: When backing up data to an external hard drive or network drive apply a password or encrypt the data so others who have access to the backup device can't open it.

Change where files save by default

If you use a Windows-based PC, the files you create in Excel will save to your Documents folder unless you browse to a different location. You may prefer to save your files in a different area of your hard drive, though, in folders you've created, and want to change this action.

1 Locate the folder to serve as the default folder on your computer.

2 If you can't see the actual path to the folder as shown here, click the down arrow to view it.

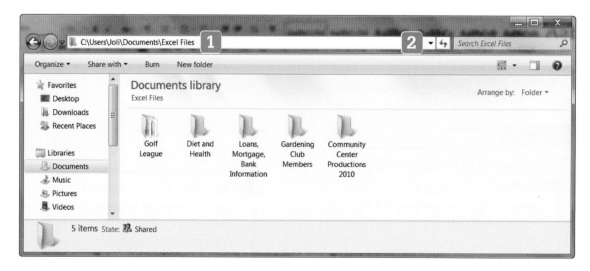

3 Highlight and copy the path.

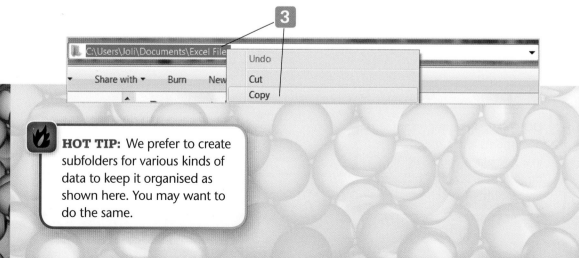

HOT TIP: We prefer to create subfolders for various kinds of data to keep it organised as shown here. You may want to do the same.

4 In Excel, click the File tab, and click Options.

5 Click Save.

6 Highlight the default save location and click Paste.

7 Click OK.

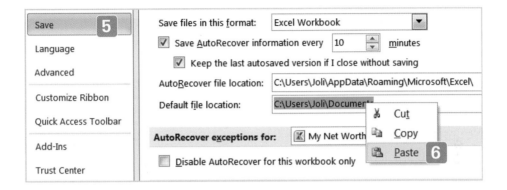

HOT TIP: If you move the default save location out of an area that is automatically backed up by your backup and restore software, make sure to back up that data manually or add the folder to the backup list.

Personalise the Quick Access Toolbar

If you have worked through this book from the beginning, you probably already know how to add icons to the Quick Access Toolbar. Unfortunately, your over-50 eyes can make the icons hard to see. If you have good eyesight, though, personalising the Quick Access Toolbar is a great way to put the commands you use most at your fingertips.

1 In Excel, click the arrow on the Quick Access Toolbar.

2 Place a tick by any icon to add.

3 To add icons for items not listed, click More Commands.

4 Select any command to add and click Add.

5 Click OK.

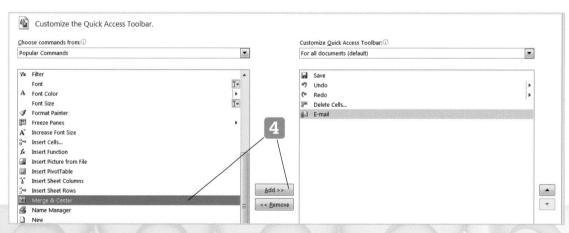

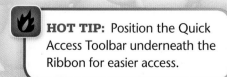 **HOT TIP:** Position the Quick Access Toolbar underneath the Ribbon for easier access.

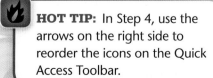 **HOT TIP:** In Step 4, use the arrows on the right side to reorder the icons on the Quick Access Toolbar.

Customise the Ribbon

You can rearrange the items on the Ribbon to suit your tastes, and you can hide items and tabs you don't use. At any time, you can reset the Ribbon to its default settings if you need to quickly access items you've hidden.

1 Right-click the Quick Access Toolbar and click Customize the Ribbon.

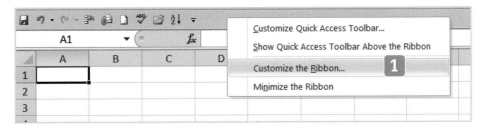

2 In the right pane, remove the tick mark by any tab, by clicking it, to hide it.

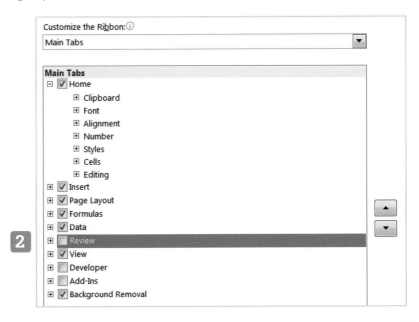

🔥 **HOT TIP:** If you have trouble seeing the Quick Access Toolbar, you can open the Customize the Ribbon dialog box from the File tab, by clicking Options.

❓ **DID YOU KNOW?**
You can create your own custom tab or custom tab group and populate it with your favourite commands. See Chapter 7.

3 Highlight (select) any tab and use the up and down arrows to reposition it on the Ribbon.

4 Expand any tab list, select any item in it, and use the up and down arrows to reposition it on the tab.

5 To remove any tab group, right-click it and click Remove.

6 Click OK.

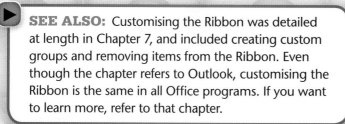

SEE ALSO: Customising the Ribbon was detailed at length in Chapter 7, and included creating custom groups and removing items from the Ribbon. Even though the chapter refers to Outlook, customising the Ribbon is the same in all Office programs. If you want to learn more, refer to that chapter.

Learn more

There's no way we could possibly cover all of what Excel has to offer in four chapters. If you'd like to learn more there are a lot of places to look.

- Click the Help icon (question mark in a circle) in Excel to access the Help files.

- Visit http://office.microsoft.com/.
- Review the other chapters in this book to learn techniques you can apply to all programs such as Cut, Copy, Paste, Format Painter, formatting, personalisation, saving and printing, and more.
- Take an intermediate or advanced course at a local community college or senior citizens centre.
- Explore advanced books that only cover Outlook.

11 Introduction to Microsoft PowerPoint

Open a new presentation	203
Explore templates	205
Preview and apply a theme	207
Add text to a slide	209
Insert a text box	211
Apply font characteristics to text	212
Insert a picture	214
Insert clip art	215
Edit a picture or clip art	217
Create a bulleted or numbered list	219
Insert a hyperlink	220
Create additional slides	221
Apply a transition	222
Preview your slideshow	223
Get Help	224

Introduction

Microsoft PowerPoint is a powerful presentation-making program that is often used in business to enhance an oral presentation. If you give presentations to clients, bosses, community leaders, associations, or committees, this may be just what you need to make your point, seal the deal, or make the sale. You can also use PowerPoint to create slideshows that run in the background while potential viewers do something else. You can create a presentation to run a product demo at a kiosk, or use a presentation to show activity schedules, lunch dates, or agenda information where applicable.

You may prefer to use PowerPoint for fun, though. You can create a presentation for a class reunion, retirement party, or birthday party, and include old pictures, quotes, music, and animations. You can create a slideshow of your children and grandchildren and use it as a type of screensaver on your computer. And just as with other Office programs, you can choose from all kinds of templates to help you get the job done quickly and easily.

Open a new presentation

When you open PowerPoint a new, blank presentation opens. There are several interface features to explore, and much of it will look familiar if you've worked through this book from the start or have worked with Office programs before. Locate the following items to familiarise yourself with the interface.

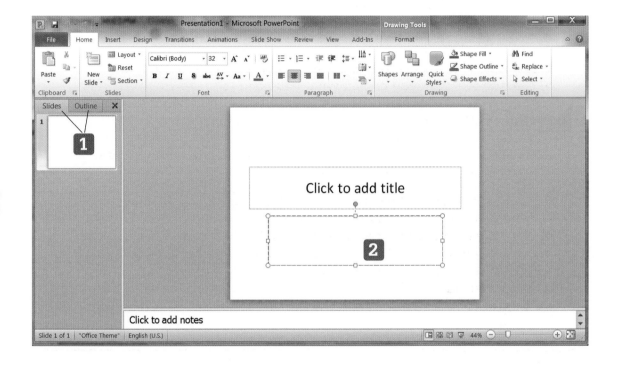

1 Slides and Outline views – initially, you'll work in Slides view. There, you can drag and drop slides to rearrange them, or click to view them.

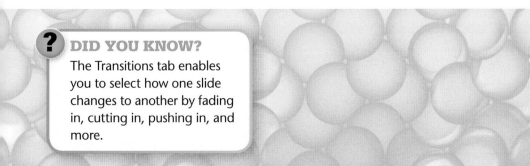

? DID YOU KNOW?

The Transitions tab enables you to select how one slide changes to another by fading in, cutting in, pushing in, and more.

2 Formatting options on the Home tab – click inside any text box to show the familiar formatting options.

3 Insert tab – click to insert pictures, shapes, clip art and other items.

4 Design tab – click to add a theme to the entire presentation with a single click.

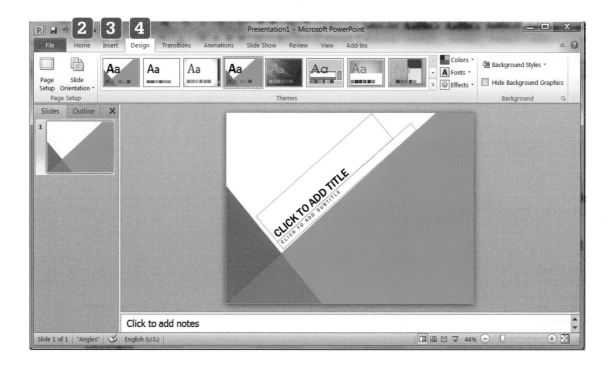

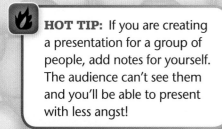

HOT TIP: If you are creating a presentation for a group of people, add notes for yourself. The audience can't see them and you'll be able to present with less angst!

DID YOU KNOW?

Notice the Zoom slider at the bottom of the page; you can use it to zoom in on your work.

Explore templates

As with Word and Excel, there are lots of templates to choose from. You'll find templates for presentations, of course, but also for award certificates, agendas, flyers, and forms (among others). When you create these items in PowerPoint you also have the option of showing them on a projector, computer monitor, or big screen if desired, without any transitional work on your part.

1 Open PowerPoint and click the File tab.

2 Click New to view the template categories.

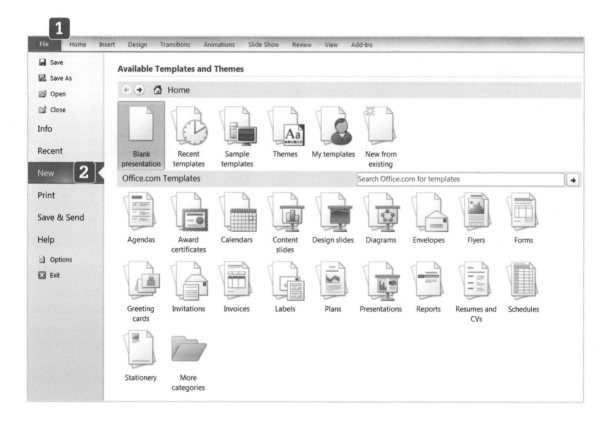

ALERT: Templates from Office.com are available online. You have to be connected to the internet to access them.

3 Click Presentations and click any category to explore (use the back arrow to return to a previous screen.)

4 Double-click any template to download it.

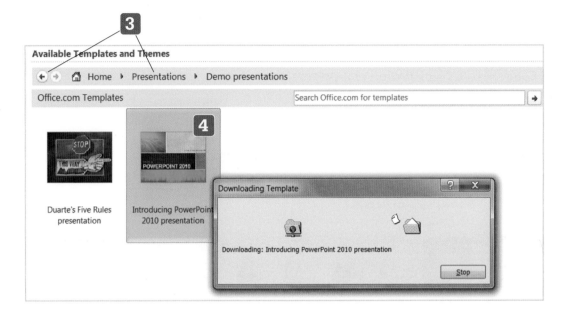

Preview and apply a theme

You can apply a theme to an entire presentation in a couple of clicks of the mouse. Themes include background colours, graphics, and preconfigured fonts, font sizes, and matching font colours. You can create a presentation quickly and easily by selecting a theme right at the beginning.

1 Open a new, blank PowerPoint presentation.

2 Click the Design tab.

3 Hover the mouse over the available themes to see their previews, and then click the arrow in the Themes group to see all of the options.

 HOT TIP: If you have trouble matching colours and fonts, or don't consider yourself the creative type, work from a theme.

? DID YOU KNOW?
When you apply a theme, it will be applied to any new slides you create for the current presentation.

HOT TIP: You can change the theme at any time, even after inputting text and images, and your data will remain intact (although its position, size, and features may change to incorporate the new theme's characteristics).

4 Drag from the bottom right corner to expand the window.

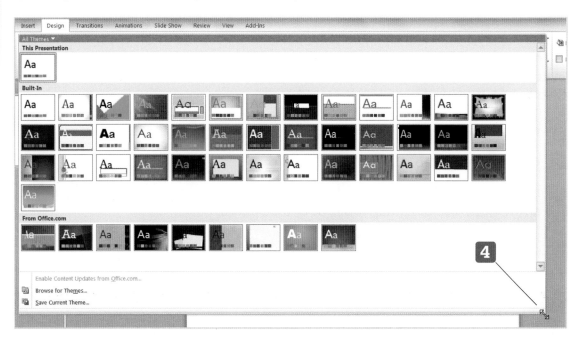

5 Click any theme to apply it.

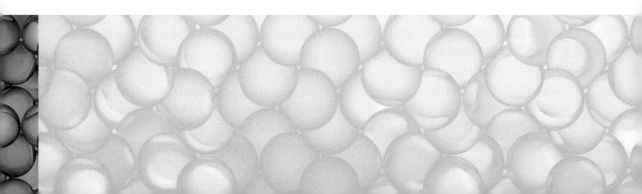

Add text to a slide

Text and pictures are the mainstays of any slide. Text is often formatted in bullets and numbered lists, although short paragraphs and quotations are certainly acceptable material. In this example we'll start with a photo album template, and input pictures and information about them.

1 Open any PowerPoint presentation. For now, consider a template.

2 Place the cursor in any text-based area of any slide. If text is already there, use your mouse to select it.

HOT TIP: Insert your digital pictures into a PowerPoint photo album template to create a slideshow to play at family reunions, birthday parties, and other family events. PowerPoint presentations make great gifts too, and can be family keepsakes if they include pictures of your family.

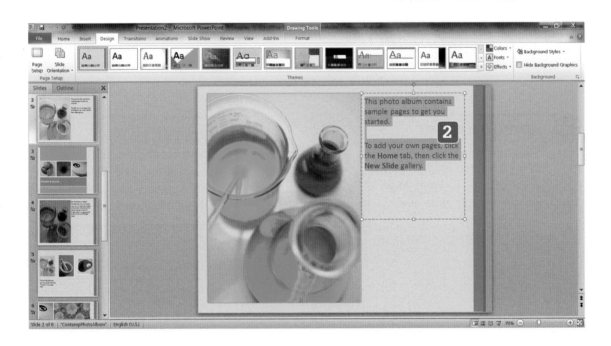

WHAT DOES THIS MEAN?

Slides: Slides are the building blocks of every PowerPoint presentation. You may recall that in the "olden days" you'd place and order 35mm physical slides in a slide sorter/presenter to create a slide presentation. These days you create virtual slides in PowerPoint.

3 Input text as desired.

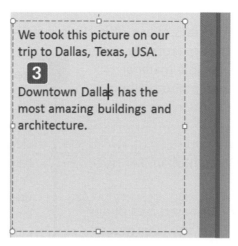

We took this picture on our trip to Dallas, Texas, USA.

3

Downtown Dallas has the most amazing buildings and architecture.

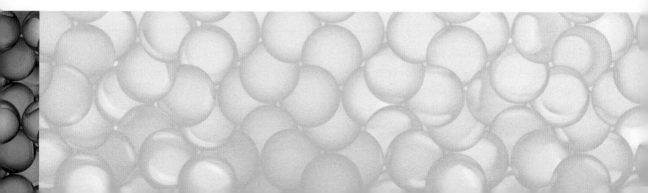

Insert a text box

When a slide does not have a text box you can insert one. Once added, simply click inside the box and type the desired text.

1 On any slide, click the Insert tab.

2 Click Text Box.

3 Click and drag with the cursor to create the box.

4 Type the desired text.

HOT TIP: You can move any text box by positioning the cursor at the top of the box so that it becomes a four-headed arrow. Then, just click and drag.

? DID YOU KNOW?
The green circle at the top of a text box enables you to rotate the box.

Apply font characteristics to text

You format text in PowerPoint the same way you format text in Word and Excel. Make your changes by selecting the text and clicking the appropriate button or list on the Home tab.

1 Select the text to format.

2 From the Home tab, select the font characteristics to apply.

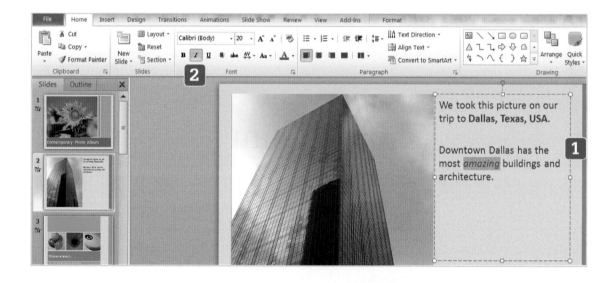

3 Explore the other formatting options, such as Convert to SmartArt.

- Click Convert to SmartArt.
- Select a design.
- Click it to apply.

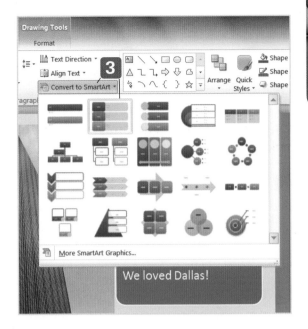

HOT TIP: You can resize any text box by dragging from the corners and sides. This will allow you to add more text, choose a larger font, or even insert other items, like clip art.

Insert a picture

You'll almost always want to insert pictures when creating slides. You may use a picture of a product for a business presentation, a picture of a person for a birthday party slideshow, or a picture from a holiday for a personal photo album.

1 To insert a picture.

- If a picture already exists as a placeholder, right-click it and select Change Picture.
- If no picture exists, click the Insert tab and click Picture.

2 Browse to the location of the picture to add and select it.

3 Click Insert.

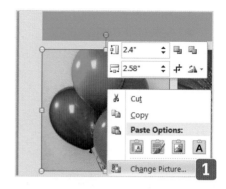

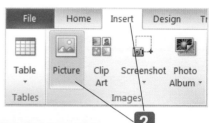

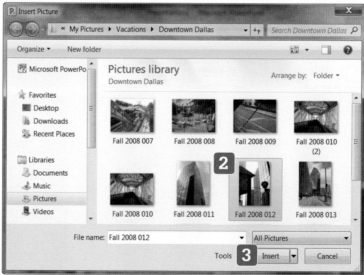

🔥 **HOT TIP:** If you're working from a template you may see instructions to 'click here' to replace a picture, but if you don't, you can right-click the picture to replace it. Alternatively, you can simply opt to delete the placeholder picture before inserting your own.

❓ **DID YOU KNOW?**
After inserting a picture a new tab will appear, Picture Tools, which will enable you to edit the picture.

Insert clip art

Clip art is digital art you obtain from various third parties on disks and online. Office comes with its own clip art, available from Office.com. You can search the clip art library to find the perfect graphic for your needs.

1 Select the slide to insert clip art into.

2 Click the Insert tab and click Clip Art.

3 In the Clip Art window, search for the desired art.

4 Double-click the art to insert it.

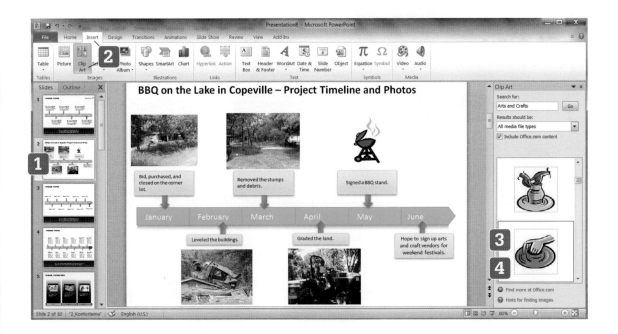

HOT TIP: To create your own graphics, insert shapes, SmartArt, charts, text boxes, WordArt and other items from the Insert tab.

5 Resize the art as needed, and use the four-headed arrow to drag the art to the proper location on the slide.

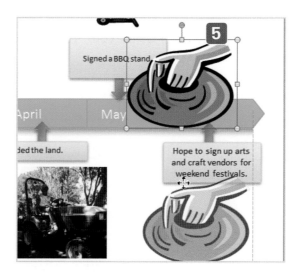

HOT TIP: If you want to put a picture on top of a shape you've drawn, select the shape and, from the Drawing Tools tab, click Send Backward, and then Send to Back.

Edit a picture or clip art

After inserting a graphic, click it to access the tools to edit it. You'll most likely need to resize it, but you may also want to put a frame around it, add artistic effects, sharpen or soften, or perform other edits.

1 Click the picture or graphic and note the new tab.

2 Click the tab. Here, that's Picture Tools.

3 Position your mouse at the corner of the graphic and drag to resize it.

4 Position your mouse at the top of the graphic and drag to position it. (You'll need the four-headed arrow to do this).

5 Browse the items on the new tab. Experiment with the following as applicable.

- Picture Styles – Click to add a frame, outline the image, or even change the image shape.

- Picture Border; Picture Effects; Picture Layout – To add a frame, add an effect, or change the shape of the picture or clip art.
- Colour; Artistic Effects; Corrections – To recolour or add effects to the image.

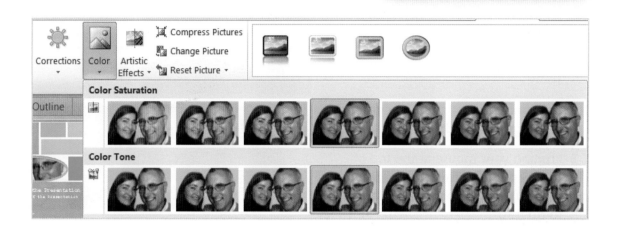

 DID YOU KNOW?
There's an option on the Picture Tools tab that enables you to rotate the picture.

 HOT TIP: From the Picture Tools tab, click Crop and Crop to Shape to create interesting graphics.

Create a bulleted or numbered list

Numbered and bulleted lists are quite helpful when presenting. They give your audience something to look at and focus on while you're speaking and expanding on the points in your slide. Students should understand these are important points and make notes; investors should have access to facts and figures; birthday party attendees should get a good laugh!

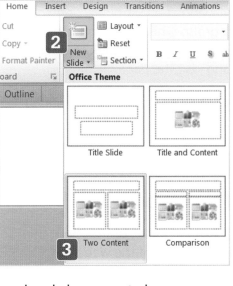

1 Click the File tab, and click New. Double-click Blank Presentation.

2 From the Home tab, click New Slide.

3 Click Two Content.

4 Click in the new slide. Note that a bullet point has already been created.

5 Type the bullet point and press Enter on the keyboard. Continue as desired.

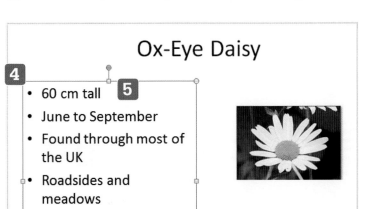

Ox-Eye Daisy

- 60 cm tall
- June to September
- Found through most of the UK
- Roadsides and meadows

 HOT TIP: When creating a presentation, stagger slides that have lists with those that don't. You wouldn't want to bore your audience!

 HOT TIP: Note the icons in the slide prior to clicking. Click an icon to add (in order from left to right) table, chart, picture, clip art, media.

Insert a hyperlink

You click a hyperlink to go to a web page. If the person viewing your presentation is doing the viewing at a computer, or if you're presenting to a group while also connected to the internet, you can click the hyperlink to open a web browser and visit the page.

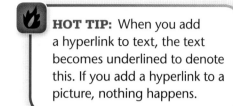

HOT TIP: When you add a hyperlink to text, the text becomes underlined to denote this. If you add a hyperlink to a picture, nothing happens.

1 To add a hyperlink to text, an image, SmartArt or other item, first select the item.

2 Right-click the item.

3 Click Hyperlink.

4 Type, paste, or browse to the location of the web site.

5 Click OK.

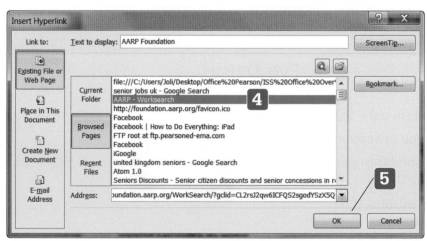

? DID YOU KNOW?

If you want to test the hyperlink to make sure you've selected the right one or configured it correctly, right-click the item and click Open Hyperlink.

HOT TIP: The surest way to input the proper hyperlink is to visit the web page and select and then copy the address in the web browser's address bar. Then you can right-click to paste the address in the Insert Hyperlink window.

Create additional slides

If you're working on a presentation from scratch (or even from a template), you'll need to insert additional slides; presentations consist of multiple slides. There are two easy ways to insert a new slide.

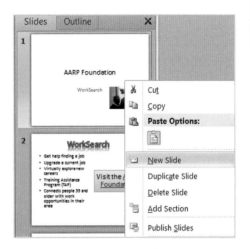

- Right-click any slide and click New Slide to insert a slide after it.
- From the Home tab, click New Slide, and select the type of slide to add.

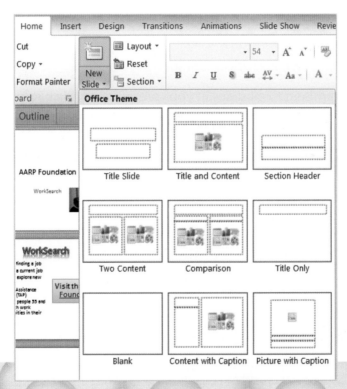

? DID YOU KNOW?

If you select a new theme from the Design tab, the options in the New Slide dropdown list will look different from the way they look here.

 HOT TIP: To move a slide, in the Slides list in the left pane, click and drag the slide to its new location.

Apply a transition

When you play your presentation as a slide show, by default there is no 'transition' when you move from slide to slide. One slide simply disappears and the next appears. You can apply a transition so that one slide dissolves into another, slips in from the left or the right, dissolves in and out, or even pans in. We think it's always good to apply a transition; it gives the presentation pizazz.

1 Click the slide to apply a transition to, and click the Transitions tab.

2 Click any transition to preview it.

3 To make the transition last longer (or to make it shorter) adjust the Duration.

4 To see more transitions, click the down arrow in the Transitions group.

5 If you want the slides to change automatically after a specific amount of time (vs. your clicking to advance them):

- Remove the tick by On Mouse Click.
- Place a tick by After, and select a time.

6 To apply this transition to all slides in your presentation, click Apply To All. Otherwise, repeat for each slide that you want to have a transition.

 HOT TIP: If you can find a presentation template you like, use it. You can always change the transitions, themes, fonts, and the like.

Preview your slideshow

You've chosen or created a theme, created and personalised slides, and even applied transitions. Now it's time to see what your first stab at a presentation looks like when you play it.

1 Click the Slide Show tab.

2 Click From Beginning. (Note you can also play from the current slide.)

3 If you set the slideshow to change slides automatically, do nothing. If you did not, you have to click the mouse to switch slides.

4 To stop a presentation, click the ESC key on the keyboard.

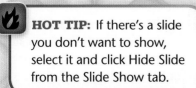 **HOT TIP:** If there's a slide you don't want to show, select it and click Hide Slide from the Slide Show tab.

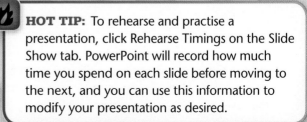 **HOT TIP:** To rehearse and practise a presentation, click Rehearse Timings on the Slide Show tab. PowerPoint will record how much time you spend on each slide before moving to the next, and you can use this information to modify your presentation as desired.

Get Help

As with any Office program you can click F1 to get to the Help pages. There you'll find helpful articles and videos, and learn how to perform basic tasks. If there's something we don't cover in this book, you can bet it'll be covered there.

1 With PowerPoint open, click F1 on the keyboard.

2 Locate and click Basic Tasks in PowerPoint 2010.

Basic tasks in PowerPoint 2010

Here are some basic tasks that you can

In this article

↓ What is PowerPoint?
↓ Find and apply a template
↓ Create a presentation
↓ Open a presentation
↓ Save a presentation
↓ Insert a new slide
↓ Add shapes to the slide
↓ View a slide show
↓ Print a presentation
↓ Tips for creating an effective presentation

3 Browse through the articles and sections.

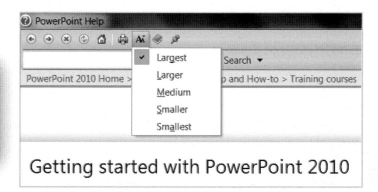

? DID YOU KNOW?

You can change the size of the font used in the Help pages from the title bar.

 HOT TIP: To rate a template you've used, with the template open, click F1. You'll have the option to rate the template there.

Top 10 Office 2010 Problems Solved

1 Find a synonym for a word   226

2 Zoom in on anything   227

3 Create a greeting card, award certificate,
   budget sheet, or anything else, fast!   228

4 Configure Outlook to check for email
   more often   230

5 Insert and delete rows and columns in
   Excel   232

6 Change default settings in Office
   programs   234

7 Resolve printing issues   235

8 Resize, edit, or reposition, pictures or
   clip art   236

9 Resolve a problem with an Excel formula   237

10 Resolve a problem that is not addressed
   here or in the book   239

Problem 1: Find a synonym for a word

You have a word on the tip of your tongue but can't come up with it, or, you've used a word too many times in a paragraph and need an alternative. This is where the Thesaurus comes in handy. Of course, you can use it when you don't know the definition of a word, too.

1 Place your cursor inside a word you'd like to find an alternative for, learn the definition of, or replace.

2 Right-click with the mouse.

3 Click Synonyms.

4 Click the word you want to use to replace the selected word or click outside the menu to cancel.

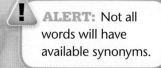
ALERT: Not all words will have available synonyms.

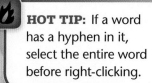
HOT TIP: If a word has a hyphen in it, select the entire word before right-clicking.

? DID YOU KNOW?
You can also access the Thesaurus from the Review tab. From here you can type a word to search for options.

Problem 2: Zoom in on anything

If you're having trouble seeing what's on the screen you know you can use the slider across the bottom to increase the page width. You can also use Zoom. Zoom lets you increase the size by a specific percentage as well as other options.

1 From the View tab in Word, Excel, and PowerPoint, click Zoom.

2 Experiment with different Zoom views, clicking OK to apply.

3 In Outlook, move the slider at the bottom of the page.

HOT TIP: If you need to zoom in on a photo or page element, set Zoom to 200% and use the scroll bars to move around in the document.

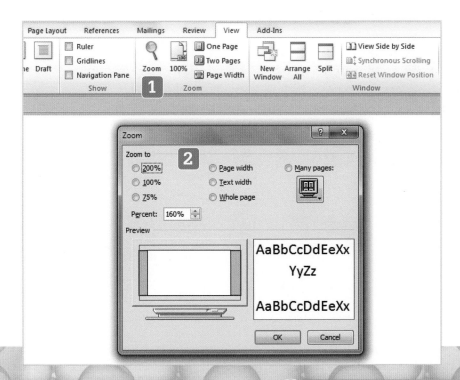

HOT TIP: If you click 75% you can often view a Word document two pages at a time; at 200% the text will take up more than the entire page.

? DID YOU KNOW?

If you have two documents open at the same time, you can view them side by side. Side by Side is an option from the View tab.

Problem 3: Create a greeting card, award certificate, budget sheet, or anything else, fast!

If you need to create something fast, consider a template. Templates are available in Word, Excel, and PowerPoint from the File tab. Just click New. You'll find templates for cards, certificates, presentations, budget sheets and more.

1 In Word, Excel, or PowerPoint, click the File tab.

2 Click New.

HOT TIP: Templates aren't just for when you're in a hurry; use templates, especially in Excel and PowerPoint, to get started on anything.

3 Under the Office.com section, browse the available template categories.

4 Double-click any subcategory. Click the Back button to return to the main categories.

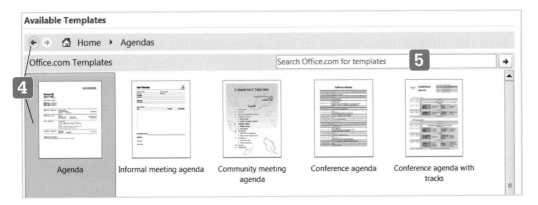

5 To find something specific, type a keyword into the Search box and click the arrow to see what's available.

HOT TIP: Printing your own greeting cards, invoices, wedding invitations, and award certificates is often much less expensive than purchasing them from a shop or printers.

Problem 4: Configure Outlook to check for email more often

Even though your children and grandchildren know you are busy and are involved in lots of activities, they still expect you to read and respond to emails immediately. This is especially true if they think (or know) you are online or at your desk.

1 Click the File tab.

2 Click Options.

3 Click Advanced and scroll to access Send/Receive (if necessary).

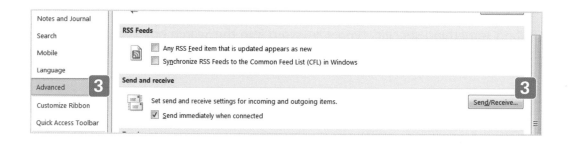

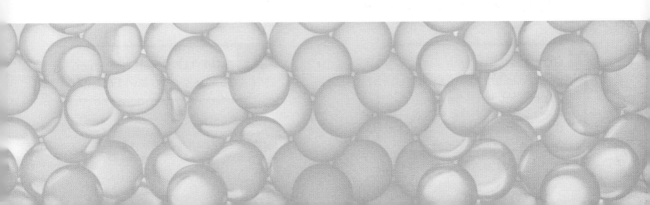

4 Click Send/Receive and change how often to check for new mail. Here it's set to 5 minutes.

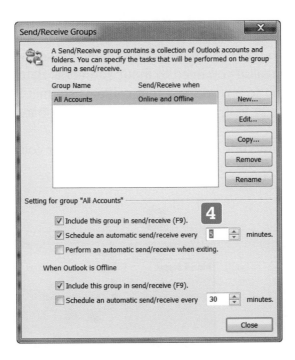

5 Click Close and then, OK.

Problem 5: Insert and delete rows and columns in Excel

There will be times when you need to insert and delete rows and columns. Generally this happens when you realise you need to input additional data after the fact, such as adding a Country column to a worksheet that contains contact information, or deleting part of a budget worksheet that doesn't apply, like student loans, child care, or rent.

1 Click the row or column title you'd like to insert a row or column in front of.

2 Right-click and select Insert.

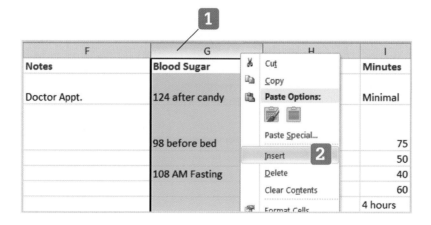

3 Name or format the new column as desired.

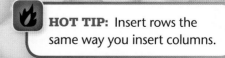

E	F	G	H
BP/Calorie Burn	Notes	Body Fat	Blood Sugar
117/72	Doctor Appt.		124 after candy

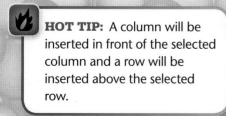

HOT TIP: A column will be inserted in front of the selected column and a row will be inserted above the selected row.

HOT TIP: Insert rows the same way you insert columns.

4 Click the row or column title to delete or hide, such as A, B, or C, or 1, 2, or 3.

M	N	O	P	Q	R	S
				4		
Thursday		Friday		Saturday		
2/21/2008		2/22/2008		2/23/2008		
	Total		Total		Total	
	0.00		0.00		0.00	
	Total		Total		Total	Total Hours
	0.00		0.00		0.00	Scheduled
0.00		0.00		0.00		6.00
0.00		0.00		0.00		0.00
0.00		0.00		0.00		0.00

5 Right-click and select Hide or Delete.

Context menu:
- ✂ Cut
- 📋 Copy
- **Paste Options:**
- 📋
- Paste Special...
- Insert
- Delete
- Clear Contents
- Format Cells...
- Column Width...
- **5** Hide
- Unhide

HOT TIP: If you insert the row or column in the wrong place, right-click the column title and click Cut, and then right-click the column title beside the desired position and click Paste.

HOT TIP: To select multiple rows or columns, hold down the Shift key while selecting those that are contiguous or the Ctrl key when selecting those that are non-contiguous.

HOT TIP: To unhide hidden rows and columns, from the Home tab, in the Cells group, click Format and then Hide and Unhide.

Problem 6: Change default settings in Office programs

When you click the File tab in any Office application and then click Options, a dialog box will appear with options you can configure for that specific program. For instance in Outlook, you can configure how often Outlook should check for new email, or how the Calendar should display your week. In all applications you can personalise the Ribbon and Quick Access Toolbar, access language options, and manage add-ins.

1 Open any Office program and click the File tab.

2 Click Options.

3 Click each tab on the left pane to see the options.

4 Read through the Advanced options.

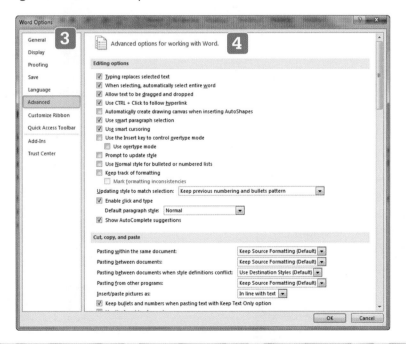

HOT TIP: Customise the Quick Access Toolbar in each Office program you use to add commands to it you access often. If you have trouble seeing the toolbar, consider customising the Ribbon instead.

HOT TIP: For Word, Excel, and PowerPoint, in Options, in Save, change where files save by default if you have created organisational folders for each program on your computer.

Problem 7: Resolve printing issues

Print Preview enables you to see how your page will look prior to printing. You can use this information to edit your presentation, choose a specific paper or size, collate, print in colour and more. In the Print window, you can also see if the printer is "online" and available, and configure options like collating copies and printing in black and white instead of colour.

1 Click the File tab.

2 Click Print.

3 Make the following decisions:
- Number of copies
- Which printer to use if more than one is available
- Which slides to print
- How many slides to print per page
- To print on one side of the page or both (if your printer offers this feature)
- To collate the copies if more than one copy is printed
- To print in colour or black and white
- To add a header or footer

4 Click Print.

> **HOT TIP:** Note in the Settings section of PowerPoint that the default is to print the entire presentation. You can opt to print the current slide or only specific slides.

> **ALERT:** The printer must be listed as "online" to use it. If it is "offline", verify it's connected to a power outlet, turned on, and connected to the computer.

> **HOT TIP:** Click Printer Properties to access additional features such as paper type, paper tray, print quality, and watermarks as applicable to your printer.

Problem 8: Resize, edit, or reposition pictures or clip art

After you've inserted a picture or clip art, you will probably find some reason to edit it. It may be too large or too small, you may want to align it with existing text, add a border, or change the brightness or contrast, to name a few issues. You access editing options from the Picture Tools tab which appears when you click the clip art or image.

1 Click the picture or clip art you inserted into the document, worksheet, email, or slide.

2 Click the Picture Tools tab.

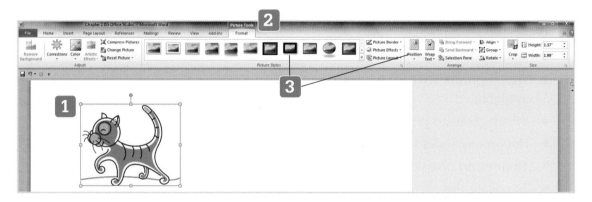

3 As applicable:

- From the Picture Styles group, click any border.
- To change how the picture aligns with the text, click Position and select any option.
- To apply an effect, click Picture Effects and explore for the desired effect.

4 Continue editing as desired.

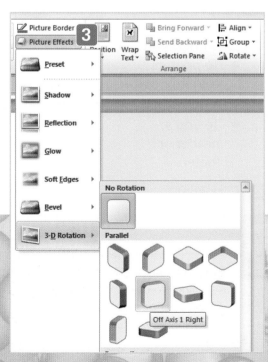

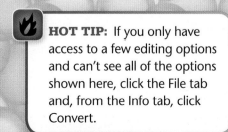

HOT TIP: If you only have access to a few editing options and can't see all of the options shown here, click the File tab and, from the Info tab, click Convert.

Problem 9: Resolve a problem with an Excel formula

When formatting goes awry in Excel, you may see all pound signs. When formulas go awry, you may get data that doesn't "add up". When there are other problems, you will see a triangle in a cell or what looks like a portion of a formula instead of data. In these instances, there is most likely an issue with the calculation or something amiss in your logic. Help is available, though.

1 If you see a triangle in a cell, click the cell. Then:

- Click the exclamation mark beside it.
- Review the information. (In this instance, we've omitted adjacent cells, which is OK.)

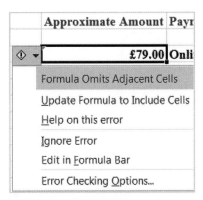

- Note the options to repair the problem. (In this case we can ignore the error.)

HOT TIP: If you can't get a formula to work, click the X next to fx in the Formula bar to delete it and try again or find another option.

2 If you see a formula in a cell:

- Click the exclamation mark if one exists. You'll then be able to review the problem and apply possible solutions.

- Click the cell to view what's missing from the formula. Often you need to specify the cells to use.

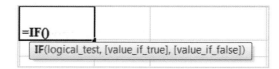

- Click the cell and click the command that appears below it. Here, you'd click If. You can then review the Help files.

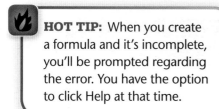

HOT TIP: When you create a formula and it's incomplete, you'll be prompted regarding the error. You have the option to click Help at that time.

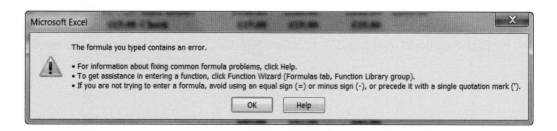

HOT TIP: If you create a formula to average a set of numbers and include cells that aren't numbers, but instead dates or text, you may still get a number, albeit an incorrect one.

Problem 10: Resolve a problem that is not addressed here or in the book

There's an icon on the far right side of each Office Ribbon that is a blue question mark. That's the Help icon. Click it to access the Microsoft Office Help files. If you're ever stuck and want a quick answer, this is the place to find it.

1 Click the blue icon on the Ribbon or press F1 on your keyboard.

2 If necessary, drag from the corner of the Help window to resize it.

3 Browse the available Help files or type a search word into the Search window.

4 Navigate the Help files as you would navigate a web page, by clicking links and using the Back and Forward buttons.

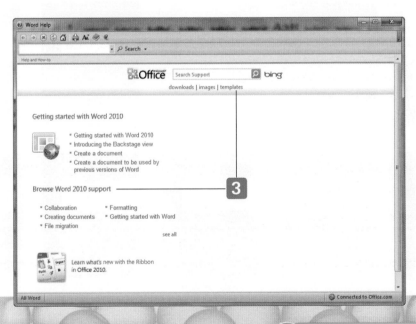

HOT TIP: To access all of the available Help files, connect to the internet. Most of the Help files are at Office.com.

? DID YOU KNOW?
At the top of the Help window is a Print icon. Click it to print any Help page or topic.

Use your computer with confidence

9780273736127

9780273736134

9780273736141

9780273736158

9780273729136

9780273723547

9780273723554

9780273736806

9780273736844

9780273723493

9780273723486

9780273729297

9780273723479

9780273736820

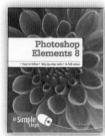
9780273734390

9780273723530

9780273734925

9780273729181

9780273729129

9780273729174

Practical. Simple. Fast.

PEARSON